"*Where Prayer Becomes Real* is not only one of the very best books on prayer I have ever read, but it is one of the most practically transformative books I have ever read, full stop. Because this is more than a book to read—this is a book that you practice, that you live, that you become. If you have ever longed for the practice of your faith to include an authentic, intimate prayer life, or if you have longed for your life to become prayer, I have no higher recommendation than these pages. Not only will I be earnestly recommending this book to anyone who wants to truly learn how to pray, but this is the book on prayer I will personally be returning to again and again, because these pages genuinely turn the soul toward intimate communion with God."

Ann Voskamp, author of the *New York Times* bestsellers
The Broken Way and *One Thousand Gifts*

"As a pastor and teacher of Scripture, I am always looking for resources that can help me and the people I serve *practice* faith versus merely talking about faith. This is especially true regarding one of the most mysterious practices of faith: prayer. In this wonderful volume, prayer is made less intimidating and mysterious on the one hand and much more compelling and accessible on the other. If you are seeking to grow in the life of prayer or are helping others do the same, *Where Prayer Becomes Real* is an excellent place to begin."

Scott Sauls, senior pastor of Christ Presbyterian Church in
Nashville, Tennessee, and author of
Jesus Outside the Lines and *A Gentle Answer*

"If you ever read a book on prayer, let it be this one! Just the word *prayer* can evoke guilt and 'never good enough' feelings. But as I read these pages, a mountain of spiritual shame lifted off my shoulders. Real prayer is possible. This book is oxygen for the soul. When it comes to the spiritual life, Coe and Strobel are trusted voices I return to again and again. They teach us that prayer isn't just something we do but is someone we are with (or, better yet, is someone with us). Anyone who desires a meaningful prayer life needs this book."

Anjuli Paschall, author of *Stay* and founder of
The Moms We Love Club

"This book gets right at the heart of the church's weakness in prayer—we don't pray from the heart. In fact, we shut down our hearts, thus killing any desire to have real communication with God. By wrapping prayer in the gospel, Coe and Strobel liberate us for communion with God. The authors drive home this message: Be yourself. Be honest. Be real. Only then will your prayer life come alive. I hope the Lord Jesus uses this book to break through centuries of calcification in prayer. I highly recommend *Where Prayer Becomes Real*."

Paul E. Miller, author of *A Praying Life* and *J-Curve*

"Whether you're new to prayer or have been praying for decades, *Where Prayer Becomes Real* offers something to enrich your friendship with God. Solidly theological, it doesn't settle for sleepy truths about God. This is a book to get you praying when you wake up, when you're angry with your spouse, when you feel disappointed, when praise is hard to come by. It's about prayer as honest, desire-full living before God—prayer that self-examines, self-discloses, and ultimately frees the self from having to be at the center of everything."

Jen Pollock Michel, author of *Surprised by Paradox* and *Teach Us to Want*

"Many books have been written about the various aspects of prayer, but this one is refreshingly perceptive. My assumptions were challenged and my hope renewed. Strobel's and Coe's leadership by example gives us a window into how the supernatural Word of God works in our hearts and inspires prayer."

Gloria Furman, author of *The Pastor's Wife* and *Treasuring Christ When Your Hands Are Full*

"God knows everything in our hearts and on our minds, so why would we struggle to talk with God about anything? But we do, and in *Where Prayer Becomes Real*, Kyle and John serve us as gracious, wise guides to praying more honestly. You'll find help here for deepening your conversational relationship with God. Thank you for writing this important book!"

Alan Fadling, president of Unhurried Living and author of *The Way of Presence*

"Prayer—conversation with the supreme animating force of space and time. Is there any act more transcendent? Is there any act more mystical and mystifying? In this book, Strobel and Coe share the practitioner's approach to demystifying prayer. What's more, they show the true nature of this foundational spiritual discipline: prayer is a means of attachment to the Divine Love, one that forms and transforms even the most chaotic soul."

Seth Haines, author of *The Book of Waking Up*

WHERE PRAYER

BECOMES REAL

WHERE PRAYER BECOMES REAL

HOW HONESTY WITH GOD TRANSFORMS YOUR SOUL

KYLE STROBEL
AND JOHN COE

BakerBooks

a division of Baker Publishing Group
Grand Rapids, Michigan

Published by Baker Books
a division of Baker Publishing Group
PO Box 6287, Grand Rapids, MI 49516-6287
www.bakerbooks.com

Printed in the United States of America

Library of Congress Cataloging-in-Publication Data
Names: Strobel, Kyle, 1978– author. | Coe, John H., author.
Title: Where prayer becomes real : how honesty with God transforms your soul / Kyle C. Strobel and John Coe.
Description: Grand Rapids, Michigan : Baker Books, a division of Baker Publishing Group, 2021. | Includes bibliographical references. |
Identifiers: LCCN 2020035434 | ISBN 9781540900777 (paperback) | ISBN 9781540901552 (casebound)
Subjects: LCSH: Prayer—Christianity.
Classification: LCC BV210.3 .S84 2021 | DDC 248.3/2—dc23
LC record available at https://lccn.loc.gov/2020035434

Published in association with Jenni Burke of Illuminate Literary Agency: www.illuminat eliterary.com.

Baker Publishing Group publications use paper produced from sustainable forestry practices and post-consumer waste whenever possible.

21 22 23 24 25 26 27   9 8 7 6 5 4 3

Kyle: To Oliver and Brighton,
who I love with all my heart.
May you *know* the place
where prayer becomes real.

John: To the late Dr. John Finch,
friend and mentor in the Holy Spirit
on my journey of learning
to pray honestly.

CONTENTS

ACKNOWLEDGMENTS

We would like to thank Biola University and Talbot School of Theology. We have been given such an incredible context to wrestle through prayer, the Christian life, and the nature of faithfulness. In particular, we are profoundly thankful for the continued support of the Institute for Spiritual Formation (ISF). Our colleagues at the Institute, faculty and staff alike, have been a blessing and an encouragement to us. We are thankful for your kindness, friendship, and grace. The Lord has been so kind to us in bringing you into our lives. We love praying with you. To the students, you are a continual gift. Thank you for giving yourself to prayer, to honesty, and to one another. Being with you at ISF is a joy.

I (Kyle) would like to thank Jamin Goggin, who is always available to bounce around ideas with and to talk through communicating biblical truths pastorally. Thank you for your friendship. James Merrick and I speak endlessly about prayer, and it continues to be a joy to do so. To the folks at Redeemer Church, thank you for your love and care. To the women at Redeemer who were willing to read the manuscript and provide feedback, thank you for your help and thoughtfulness. I am thankful to be part of such a *prayerful* church. Being with you has been a real joy. Finally, my wife, Kelli, is such a gift to me, and she deserves special thanks for reading and giving feedback on this book. It is better because you gave yourself to it. I'm so thankful for you. Along with Kelli, my children, Brighton and Oliver, fill my prayers with thankfulness. Brighton, thank you for supporting me through your love of books. May you seek the Lord as voraciously as you read! Oliver, who always wants to pray, may the Lord take you into the deepest places to pray, and may you know his mercy there. I would also like to thank my sister, Alison, who read drafts for us, along with my mother and father for their continued support. In particular, I had my mom in mind all during the writing process. Thank you for always praying.

I, John, would like to thank my wife, Greta. You have been my dearest friend and partner for the past forty-five years in learning how to pray and walk open to the Spirit in the Christian life. These last years in particular have taken us on a journey of prayer beyond what we experienced in our younger days. To my whole family, may the Lord bless you for all you have taught me regarding prayer, joy, love, and life.

Special thanks go to those who assisted in the production of this volume. Our fearless agent, Jenni Burke, and the good folks at Illuminate Literary Agency have been continually encouraging and helpful. Your support is greatly appreciated. Several students helped in various ways with editing and formatting, and we are grateful for their service—in particular, Ellen Balzun and Jenn Lindsey. To all the good folks at Baker, from Brian Thomasson to the whole team in marketing, design, and editing. It has been great to work with you. Thank you for your excitement about this project and your continued support.

INTRODUCTION

An Invitation to Love

If you want a boring prayer life, spend it trying to be good in prayer rather than being honest.

For a good portion of our Christian lives, prayer did not make much sense. But that wasn't our main problem. Our problem was that we weren't being honest about it. We *pretended* that prayer made sense, but it didn't. Prayer was dry, boring, and, while we're being really honest, something we avoided at all cost. Prayer at meals was fine. A quick prayer for others was great. But being with God in the deep realities of life felt like wandering in a desert. Oddly, we never considered telling God how alienating prayer seemed.

But then we heard good news: "For we do not know how to pray as we should, but the Spirit Himself intercedes for us with groanings too deep for words" (Rom. 8:26 NASB). We don't know how to pray. That is what God wants us to know about ourselves. But this is not something to despair. This is not a reason to stop praying. This is an invitation.

Have you ever received an invitation to something you really didn't want to go to? Do you remember looking at it with a bit of dread, wondering how to turn it down? Think about how different it is receiving an invitation you have been longing for. This book is an invitation, one we hope you've been yearning for. Inscribed on this invitation is the Word of the Lord:

> The LORD is near to all who call on him,
>> to all who call on him in truth. (Ps. 145:18)

This book is an invitation to embrace God's love in the truth of who you really are. Embracing God's love is allowing that love to guide you in prayer and trusting that even though you don't know how to pray as you ought, God knows and understands. He is inviting you to him in truth, to know and be known. This is an invitation to a journey with the Lord to discover that kind of prayer.

The Journey of Prayer

Like we do with all journeys, we have to start where we actually are. This simple fact is so important that it cannot be overstated. Unfortunately, most of us have never thought about where our journey of prayer has taken us. We are told where we should be and where we should go, but this isn't helpful until we can locate ourselves on the map.

Pause for a moment to consider this. If you could break down your Christian life into seasons (for some of us there will be many, and for others maybe only one or two), what did prayer look like in each season? Consider what kind of adjectives describe your praying in each season. For some, words like *exciting*, *loving*, and *joyful* might be the first to come to mind. For others, words like *lonely*, *abandoned*, *guilt-ridden*, or *boring* come to the fore. The point here is not to judge this but to be open to the truth. The goal is to know where you have been so you can follow where the Lord is leading you now.

For just a moment, sit with that and focus on what you are presently experiencing in your prayer life. Don't try to fix anything;

just be open to the truth for a moment—and share this with God. That is the beginning of prayer.

Take some time to consider what expectations you had about prayer in these seasons. Were there times when you had great expectations for prayer? Were there seasons where you had no expectations? What did you do when your expectations were not met? What are your expectations right now? Share that with God—pray.

Invitation to prayer. Throughout this book, we will be providing spaces to talk with God. These are not suggestions to simply think about or ponder. We are inviting you to stop reading and pray as prompted. It is not enough to learn *about* prayer; we want you to bring these ideas to God. On this journey of prayer, we have to pray and take our experience of prayer to God.

So we encourage you, right now, to pray about how you have *experienced* prayer in your life. How have your experiences shaped how you understand what prayer will be like? Ask the Lord to reveal to you what you bring to prayer. Ask the Lord to guide you into the truth of what is going on in your heart. This is an invitation into love: to speak the truth of your soul to the God who loves you in the deepest places of your heart.

Regardless of how we have felt about prayer, and how well or poorly we think we have done, it is important to see that the Lord has been leading us all along. He has been leading us to himself in truth. Our failure to pray, our fears that we have prayed poorly, or even our resistance to prayer are all echoes of God's invitation to pray. How can we be present to God in this? We cannot lose if we come as we are, so this is where we begin. This is the entrance to the place of deep prayer.

Deeper Prayer

To embrace deeper prayer, we must rest on how far God has gone to call us to himself to hear the truth of our hearts. God knows we do not know how to pray as we ought. That is good news! But

God does not leave us in ignorance. He leads us into truth. This journey takes us where we have not been before and where we could not go on our own. Along this road we will see things we tend to avoid, because we have not yet learned how to pray in full. But deep prayer is prayer in the truth of what is going on in our lives. That means we are called to pray from that honest place in our heart that each of us knows but only visits when something (usually) beyond our control awakens us to these realities. It is in that honest place with God where prayer becomes real.

As Margery Williams depicts in her beloved children's story *The Velveteen Rabbit*, the process of becoming "real" often entails a journey we did not expect—a journey that feels more like being worn out than becoming something new. But something new is made through this journey of love. This is the reality of prayer. As the Skin Horse tells the Velveteen Rabbit in the nursery,

> "Real isn't how you are made," said the Skin Horse. "It's a thing that happens to you. When a child loves you for a long, long time, not just to play with, but REALLY loves you, then you become Real."
>
> "Does it hurt?" asked the Rabbit.
>
> "Sometimes. . . . It doesn't happen at once," said the Skin Horse. "You become. It takes a long time. That's why it doesn't happen often to people who break easily, or have sharp edges, or who have to be carefully kept. Generally, by the time you are Real, most of your hair has been loved off, and your eyes drop out and you get loose in your joints and very shabby. But these things don't matter at all, because once you are Real you can't be ugly, except to people who don't understand."[1]

Becoming real was a confusing journey that, at times, hurt; a journey where love meant losing one's fur and being made shabby yet, at the same time, sturdier. This is the reality of prayer. In the truth of our hearts, we discover that the Spirit of the Lord is already in those places, groaning in our souls, beckoning us to follow him into truth. Prayer only truly becomes real if it follows the Spirit into these places, discovering his love precisely where we need it.

What this journey of prayer reveals is that it is about the *deep* in all of us. As the psalmist calls out to God, wondering why God has seemed to forget him, he says, "Deep calls to deep" (Ps. 42:7). Most of us do not know exactly what that means, but we resonate with it. It calls to our souls. It calls to who we really are, to the honest part of us. We know something within us must come out to meet God. The longer we are Christians, the more we recognize this, maybe even long for it, but are unsure if we are willing to embrace it. Regardless of this uncertainty in ourselves, this journey of prayer is all about love. Only love can guide us into the deep places of our souls, to attend honestly with God in the truth of ourselves before him. Only love can sustain this honesty in the life of prayer.

God is inviting us to a deeper life of prayer. Like marriage, prayer is not something we can "master" by learning the right techniques, the right words to say, or the right tone to take. We may need to learn these things, for the sake of being with our spouse well, but they won't fix anything. Like marriage, prayer is growth within a union of love where we experience, at times, conflict or harmony between what we want and what they want. In marriage, we are called not to simple "fixes" but to a journey of love that will grow and develop as we enter more deeply in love and union. This, too, is the journey of prayer.

Accepting the Invitation to Pray

You can read this book in two ways. Which one you choose will depend on your personality and what you know about how you tend to read and comprehend. We have written this book in a specific order for a reason—to help you first understand the nature of prayer and how you have been praying before turning to practical forms of prayer. But for some, it may prove helpful to begin with the practical and then go back to the beginning. If this is you, we encourage you to read through part 2, then go back and read starting with chapter 1, and continue through the book. That way you can have the whole in mind when you go back to read through the more practical chapters in part 2.

Regardless of which path you take, we encourage you to do it prayerfully. If you accept this invitation to seek the place where prayer becomes real, remember to receive it as an invitation into love. Prayer becomes real in the unending love of your heavenly Father to know you in truth, but it is an invitation you must accept. Our invitation to you is to give yourself to the prayer exercises at the end of each chapter. Take some time to be alone in a quiet place and be still before your God. It may prove helpful to have a journal or to sit with a biblical passage or two from each chapter, and then use the exercise to pray.

One final point. We will often use "we" or "I" to refer to both of us, Kyle and John, since our experiences were so similar and so we could use pronouns that seem most natural for the context. However, occasionally we will say "I (Kyle)" or "I (John)" when we are making some point unique to the particular person. We hope this will not be too cumbersome for the reader.

PRACTICE

Knowing Our Story of Prayer

After you finish each chapter, there will be a prayer exercise like this one. Set aside some time for these, taking whatever was in the chapter and how you experienced it to the God who knows you and loves you. You may want to bring a journal to write out what is going on in your heart or you might want to take some time to rest before beginning. Regardless, we ask that you set aside time and space to enter into this meaningfully, and we hope this will be the space where the content of the book is explored with God.

. . . . .

Pause for a moment and consider the different seasons of your Christian life, however many or few there may be. Try to name each stage. Ask the Lord what seasons he has led you into and through. If you find it helpful, write them down.

You may clearly see a stage of youthfulness, filled with zeal and excitement but maybe less wisdom and patience. Then you may see a period of adolescence as you learned more about the Christian life, Scripture, and service. Maybe some seasons felt like Israel's wandering in the desert—seasons of dryness, wondering where God is. Maybe you experienced seasons of walking away and abandoning your faith for a time. Whatever you see in your own history, enter into each one of those seasons in prayer.

Pray for each season: "Father, what was it like, in this season, to be with you? What did my prayers become when I was in this place? Was I being honest with you? Was I trying to perform in prayer? Was I wondering where you were but did not think you wanted to hear me tell you that? Was I feeling alone, sad, or unmotivated but not thinking you wanted me to say those things?"

What did it look like for you to depend on God in seasons of joy or seasons of pain? Were you tempted to use prayer to control things? Whatever your experience, ask the Lord to help you see how it shaped what prayer has become for you. You may be hoping prayer will become clear and no longer confusing. Regardless of what was true in each season, share this with the Lord, and let him teach you in the reality of that place.

PART 1

What We Need
to Unlearn
about Prayer

1

What If a Wandering Mind Is a Gift?

Have you ever wondered if you were bad at prayer? Have you wondered if others understood something about prayer that you didn't? Have you ever promised God that you will try harder in prayer, only to discover you really can't? If so, you are in good company.

Some people seem born to pray. They exude delight at the chance to remain in prayer, petition, and praise. For others—for ourselves—prayer has been a struggle. Prayer has never come easy for us. Folks like us have a tendency to place conversation with God on the periphery of the Christian life (or we just ignore it and come to believe it is for only those rare few who find it to be more "natural").

The problem was that we knew we were supposed to pray and would hear sermons, read books, and listen to others talk about prayer in a way we wished to experience it, and then guilt would drive us to once again wrestle with prayer. Prayer was something we knew we should do, and we did it as an act of obedience, but we failed to be honest about how difficult it was. Why? Because it didn't seem to work like we wanted it to or expected it *should*. This made it difficult to face the fundamental fissure in our faith: prayer sounded good as an ideal but felt bad and confusing in reality.

When Prayer Becomes Lifeless

When I (Kyle) was working on a Bible degree in college, I came to a disconcerting realization. While my knowledge of Scripture was growing exponentially, I wasn't experiencing a parallel growth in prayer. Rather, even after entering into ministry positions, and even while I was increasingly seen as a spiritual leader, I found prayer to be a lonely, confusing place. I could wrap my mind around the task of wrestling through Scripture. And even more, when I wrestled with Scripture, I had a sense of accomplishment and validation about what I was giving myself to. I was doing good devotional work. But prayer rarely felt meaningful. Rather, if I did sit down to pray, I often felt like I was pleading into an abyss—like my prayers were bouncing off the ceiling and reverberating off my dorm room walls.

Looking back, prayer felt more like talking to myself than to God. I would sometimes fall asleep while "praying" and then feel guilty that I couldn't stay awake. In response, I spent as much time trying to get my act together as I did asking for forgiveness for being so bad at prayer! If I wasn't sleeping, my mind was wandering, and, once again, prayer became a time to navigate my guilt. *Why am I so bad at prayer?* became the question that plagued me. I began to wonder if I just wasn't cut out for prayer. *Maybe I'll just keep learning the Bible and leave prayer to the experts*, I thought. Prayer mirrored all the things I didn't want to see about myself, so it was easier to focus on things that made me feel like I was growing. As a Bible student, that meant learning Scripture, but it can easily be anything that makes us feel like we're "doing better" at the Christian life.

It wasn't until seminary that I finally began to see the deeper and more profound problems with my approach to prayer. It was the words of John Coe, my coauthor for this book and former professor, that struck me deep in my heart. "Prayer is not a place to be good," he told me. "It is a place to be honest." Up until that point, I had spent the bulk of my Christian life trying to be good in prayer. Prayer was a place to stand before God and perform, and I was failing miserably. It was like a dream where you are sitting at a grand piano, ready to play for a sold-out stadium, and only then realize that you don't know how to play piano. No one signs up for that. But my problem went beyond not knowing how to pray. I ceased to pray because I thought God wanted me to prove my worth in his presence. That is where prayer goes to die.

To resurrect my prayer life, I needed to understand that Christ and the Spirit have created a place for me to pray in the presence of the Father. They have called me their own, so, like Jesus in Gethsemane or the Spirit in my heart, I can pray the truth of who I am to the God who knows, sees, and understands. This is why

Prayer is not a place to be good, it is a place to be honest.

Prayer is not a place to perform, it is a place to be present.

Prayer is not a place to be right, it is a place to be known.

Prayer is not a place to prove your worth, it is a place to receive worth and offer yourself in truth.

My wandering mind is what helped my lifeless prayer die. It taught me where my heart truly is and what my treasures really are. It taught me that I would rather not pray, but even more so, that I could not pray on my own apart from the Spirit. But I couldn't possibly see this until I came out of hiding and named the truth of my experience. Unfortunately, few of us have been *taught* these truths. Most of us learn, even if no one ever taught us explicitly, that what God wants from us in prayer is to pray *correctly*, *to pray well*. But praying in this way is a performance, a performance seeking applause and validation rather than God himself.

Prayer beyond Performance

One evening when I was in seminary, a bunch of my classmates and I went to a professor's house. The professor was talking about a pet peeve of his: when people pray to the wrong person of the Trinity, thanking the Father for dying for them, etc. After a short rant, he suggested we close in prayer. No one spoke a word! After a minute or two, everyone started laughing because we all knew what was going on. We had become so self-conscious about praying correctly and performing well that no one wanted to pray.

While this professor's hang-up about the Trinity is not an issue most people probably worry about, it is all too easy to focus on praying the right way to the detriment of actually praying. But once again, this is where prayer goes to die. If prayer becomes a place where the focus is on "doing it right," then you won't actually "do it" at all. If our prayer becomes a time when we perform, then we will judge it based on how well we stayed awake, how focused our mind was, or if we got through our list of things to pray for. If prayer becomes a place to pray about what we think God wants us to and not what is on our hearts, then we simply won't do it. It won't be real. Perhaps the deeper reality is that the heart knows when we don't pray the truth, and we get bored by our cleaned-up fantasy. In the words of Herbert McCabe, "People often complain of 'distractions' during prayer. Their mind goes wandering off on to other things. This is nearly always due to praying for something you do not really much want; you just think it would be proper and respectable and 'religious' to want it."[1]

When prayer becomes a kind of performance, it is easy to interpret experiences like having our mind wander as failures. Most of us interpret this as "not doing it right," and our natural response is to either try harder or give up. But McCabe touches on something much more profound, pointing to where a deeper life of prayer begins. Because we have the Spirit of God in our souls, mind wandering should not be seen as a random act of an undisciplined intellect. Our minds wander because, in Jesus's words, "where your treasure is, there your heart will be also" (Matt. 6:21). When we come into God's presence in prayer, we do so with the Spirit present to the deepest depths of our hearts. We should not be surprised that the truth of our hearts begins to percolate and rise to the surface. To McCabe's point, our hearts are telling us what we really long for, and the Spirit is awakening our longings to ground us in the truth of where we should be praying. When our minds wander to our finances, our job, our need for a job, our spouse, our desire for a spouse, or our worries—these are the "treasures" of the heart. These are the desires that float to the surface in God's presence. The Lord knows the heart, and as we ask him to "search us," our hearts reveal the deep desires we are to bring to him (Ps. 139:23–24).

So instead of seeing a wandering mind as a failure to pray as we ought, we should see this as an opportunity to pray about the deep longings of our souls. Mind wandering is a gift; by it, the Lord shows us the treasures of our hearts. Our call is to bring this to the Lord, who meets us in the truth of ourselves as ones who need grace and mercy in these very places.

We are tempted to do the opposite. When our minds wander in prayer, our temptation is to stop praying and start talking to ourselves. This self-talk is like pressing a "pause button" on prayer, as if we could put God on hold (whatever that means!) to try to convince ourselves to focus better in prayer. Sometimes this means chastising ourselves for not being good enough, sometimes it means wrestling with ourselves over why we couldn't focus more, and the list could go on and on.

Much of "prayer" can become talking *to ourselves* about what is going wrong, about where our minds are wandering to, and about how bad and confused we may feel about our relationship with God. In those moments, we pause our talking with God because we do not think these are the kinds of things God wants to talk about. They are *our* problems. They represent *our* wandering minds and hearts toward idols, worries, and loves. I often find my mind wandering to things I can control, like my calendar, my work, and things I want to do around the house. Whereas God's presence makes me feel out of control and, oftentimes, guilty, these things make me feel in control and better about how I am doing in life. I now watch where my mind goes so I can bring these things to God.

I can pray, "Father, look at this. Look at what my heart does in your presence. Lord, deep in my heart I long for control to calm my fears, my worries, and all my anxieties. Lord, help me trust you with these. I believe, Lord. Help me here in my unbelief to really know—to deeply know—that my life is most secure in your hands and not my own."

Rather than turning against myself in prayer, admonishing myself to "be better," I now use my wandering mind as an opportunity to be with him. We have to avoid trying to fix our lives or giving ourselves a pep talk on how to rightly talk with God when we pray. That is not what prayer is, and this is not where our hope is found. Prayers become boring and lifeless when we wrestle with ourselves in our guilt, anxiety, fear, or shame rather than bring them to God. That's why we stop praying!

Learning to Speak the Truth

It wasn't until I saw what I was doing in prayer and realized how much of my prayer life had become wrestling with myself and my guilt that I was finally able to receive the good news of prayer. It was in that place, feeling like a failure at the Christian life, that God revealed my strategies of hiding, failure, and sin. In pouring out my heart to the Lord, I came to experience the love of God in a way I had never known. It dawned on me that in much of my prior prayer life, I had not really believed that God was interested in the deep (and often embarrassing) realities of my heart. Somewhere along the way I had come to think that God was interested only in things that were good, religious, clean, moral, and tidy. Therefore, I wanted to be good *in* prayer and good *at* prayer.

The lie we are tempted to believe and perpetuate in our prayers is that God is interested in only well-kept sorts of things rather than the truth. But in reality, God loves the believer precisely in those sins and failures. It was in those sins that Christ died for us (Rom. 5:8). God was not afraid of our sin and mess; we were. In our fear, we did not talk about the deep pains and sins with God, so our zeal for prayer slowly died.

Like Jesus's conversation with the woman at the well who wanted to talk about social and religious customs while Jesus addressed her scandalous sex life (John 4:1–26), prayer is an invitation into truth because truth gets us to the real desires of our hearts. Or, in Jesus's words,

> Two men went up into the temple to pray, one a Pharisee and the other a tax collector. The Pharisee, standing by himself, prayed thus: "God, I thank you that I am not like other men, extortioners, unjust, adulterers, or even like this tax collector. I fast twice a week; I give tithes of all that I get." But the tax collector, standing far off, would not even lift up his eyes to heaven, but beat his breast, saying, "God, be merciful to me, a sinner!" I tell you, this man went down to his house justified, rather than the other. For everyone who exalts himself will be humbled, but the one who humbles himself will be exalted. (Luke 18:10–14)

The tax collector prayed in truth—opening his heart to the Lord and throwing himself on the mercy of God. This man used the deep worries and fears of his heart to come into God's presence, whereas the Pharisee used his religious life to keep prayer tidy and detached from the messy truths of his heart.

All of this raises some questions about our own prayer lives. Are you praying about the real desires of your heart, or has prayer become a place to recite the "right" things to want? Where did you learn what you could and couldn't pray about? Where did these notions come from?

Take a moment right now to ask God about this. Many Christians have come to believe that God wants them to clean up their sin before he will accept their prayer. The only time they pray about sin, therefore, is when they repent and ask for forgiveness. If this is you, what if you also brought your underlying desire for sin to God? You can pray, "Lord, look at how much I long for money and security in this world. Father, when I snapped at my wife today, what was driving that in me? Why do I long to be in control and have life on my terms? Lord, be with me in my anger, lust, and envy. Know me in these sins, Lord, and help me bring them to you."

When we believe God cannot, or simply will not, hear about our sin and failure, we end up keeping these truths to ourselves. But we are not able to manage our sin. We need to bring it to him. When we come to God with our petitions and our minds are whispering, *Oh, John, you are asking God with such little fervor and love!* or *Oh, Kyle, you are so out of it today, get your act together!* we have to learn how to bring these to God. Do we believe God can hear these kinds of things? We know the Spirit of Christ hears and sees all that we are wrestling with and is calling us to share that with him. Hear his call: "Come to me, all who labor and are heavy laden, and I will give you rest. Take my yoke upon you, and learn from me, for I am gentle and lowly in heart, and you will find rest for your souls. For my yoke is easy, and my burden is light" (Matt. 11:28–30).

Prayers of a Fallen Heart

When we considered how our own prayer lives developed, we realized that we avoided prayer if we felt like we were not doing well with God. This mostly had to do with whether we felt good about our devotional lives. If we were struggling with a specific sin, we would focus on getting our act together *before* bringing the sin to God. Or, more accurately, we tried to get the right attitude toward the sin before we talked with God about it. We were still trying to know God in our devotional goodness rather than in the broken reality of our lives. It did not dawn on us to come to him in our weakness, sharing what we were feeling and opening our hearts to him.

Instead of being with God in truth, we were trying to manage our sin and our relationship with him. Like the Pharisee in the temple, we were using prayer to mirror our goodness back to us, and when we couldn't, we simply avoided praying. Because of this, prayer became a burdensome yoke that made us dread doing it rather than an easy yoke where we came to find the waters of life.

Like Adam and Eve in fig-leaf clothes hiding from God behind shrubs, we may experience a grave temptation to let the Christian life become about managing God rather than being with him. Somewhere on the journey of faith, we came to believe that even though we can do nothing without Christ Jesus (John 15:5), what he really wants is for us to get our acts together and then show him how well we have done. Somehow we came to believe that even though he cried out from the cross, "It is finished," what he really meant is that he wants us to be good. Many believe Christ has atoned for their sins yet still beat themselves up in prayer to try to atone for their sins themselves to placate his wrath. But this is Christ's work and not ours. There is a better way—a deeper way— and it is a journey into a profound life of prayer, honesty, and love.

Our mind wandering is a gift because it reveals the deep truth in us that the Lord already sees and knows. It is always a gift to be known in truth by our Lord, because we follow a God who abides in steadfast love and mercy. The goal of prayer is never to conquer or silence a distracted mind. Rather, it is to be with God in truth—to offer ourselves to be known and received by the One who knows.

PRACTICE

Prayer When Our Minds Wander

Take a moment to sit with the Lord. Affirm the truth that he is God and you are not, that he knows and sees all, and that you want to be with him. Pray the words of David from Psalm 27:4–5 and watch what goes on in your heart:

> One thing have I asked of the Lord,
>   that will I seek after:
> that I may dwell in the house of the Lord
>   all the days of my life,
> to gaze upon the beauty of the Lord
>   and to inquire in his temple.
>
> For he will hide me in his shelter
>   in the day of trouble;
> he will conceal me under the cover of his tent;
>   he will lift me high upon a rock.

Offer yourself to God.

As you open your heart to the Lord, be watchful (Col. 4:2). What does your heart do? Can you simply be with your Lord? If so, praise God and be thankful. If your mind starts wandering, don't reject or try to control it. First, share these things with the Lord—share all the things on your heart. He sees them and knows the truth better than we do.

Then, secondly, ask him, "Lord, what is this desire of my heart? What does my heart treasure more than being with you?" As you are watchful of your heart in his presence, do not fear the truth. If your mind wanders to your worries or your weekly calendar, then be open with the Lord about why your heart turns to these places. Do you feel like you don't have control in God's presence, so you turn to something you can control? Do you feel like prayer isn't productive, so you turn to something that is? Talk to God about these matters.

Allow your heart to unveil the deep loves of your soul and hold them up to God. Mentally take them in your hands and offer them to him. Know that he is enough for you here. Know that it was in your sin that Christ died for you (Rom. 5:8). Know that there is now no condemnation for those in Christ Jesus (Rom. 8:1). Allow your heart to respond to God's kindness in the midst of your brokenness. Ask the Lord to teach you about the treasures of your heart and guide you in wisdom.

2

What If Prayer Can Be a Place to Avoid God?

When I (Kyle) was little, probably around five or six, I remember asking my mom a question that had been rattling around my little soul. "Mom, since Jesus tells us to love our enemies and to pray for them, should we pray for Satan?" My poor mother, not quite sure what to do with my inquiry, just assured me that I needn't worry about praying for Satan. I can remember back to that moment, and I recall a real tension and worry in my heart. Someone had read me Matthew 5:44–45, which states, "But I say to you, Love your enemies and pray for those who persecute you, so that you may be sons of your Father who is in heaven." When I heard this passage, I became incredibly anxious. I was worried that if I didn't pray in the right way, then I couldn't become a child of my heavenly Father. I didn't bother asking God about it, because I assumed God only heard my prayers if I prayed the "right sorts of things" (and that is what I was trying to figure out!). I didn't yet understand prayer as a place to be with God, as much as a place where I did the right things to get what I wanted. This is not surprising for a child, but, unfortunately, things didn't mature much in my prayer life when I grew older.

After the first sin, Adam gave God a speech in the garden, not to be with him but to manage and try to manipulate him (Gen. 3:9–12). Eventually, God gave his people a temple and a sacrificial system to be with him, but rather than using it that way, they tried to use it as a means to control him. This is the continual temptation of the human heart. Perhaps the most difficult reality to embrace as Christians is that our devotional lives are the headquarters of our rebellion. Our sin works itself out in our devotion, which is why the garden and the temple both became sites to manage God rather than be with him. This is why Jesus rebuked the Pharisees so harshly but tended to be much kinder to those who saw their brokenness and sin for what it was. They prayed the truth in their sin and brokenness, and they sought help where it can be found—in God. We, however, are tempted to think our spiritual practices are somehow purified, and we fail to realize we can use spiritual practices to keep God at bay.

When I grew older and my prayers still hadn't matured, it became clear to me that I didn't see God's presence as good news in my sin and brokenness. Instead, I felt like a child under discipline who needed to either go away or do something good until I could pray as I was supposed to. I didn't understand the good news of prayer, so prayer became a place to avoid God, or try to manipulate him. To understand how prayer is a gift, we have to embrace the forgiveness and love of the Lord. We have to see how God meets us in our brokenness, rebellion, and sin with good news.

The Christian Life in Miniature

Our prayer life is our Christian life miniaturized. What we believe about life with God reveals itself in how we pray. This is why it is helpful to consider what our approach to prayer has been—to see the deep beliefs about God we are not even aware of. If we believe the Christian life is primarily about being good, then prayer will be a time to try to be good (or, if nothing else, a time to try to project your goodness *at* God). Maybe we pray only for others, so that when we finish praying, we can look back at how faithful we have been and feel like we are doing well as Christians. Maybe we pray only short prayers so we don't have time to experience our mind wandering, falling asleep, or any of the other things that can make prayer so humbling.

Alternatively, we may think the Christian life is primarily about knowing true things about God. When this happens, prayer becomes a time to verbalize our right beliefs. We focus on naming the truth about God but avoid the truth of our hearts because it feels unnerving and counterproductive. We opt to pray the truth *at* God, assuming in our hearts that these truths are met with God's Fatherly approval. But the Christian life is not primarily about being good or knowing true things (although it should, of course, include these). Rather, the Christian life is about abiding in Christ, thereby sharing in the life of the Father so we may share *our* life with the Father. Therefore, we must be open to ways that our devotion, worship, and even service to God can be used to avoid him.

As the Christian life in miniature, prayer should flow naturally out of the good news of our salvation. In faith, we trust that prayer is not something we have to create or somehow generate on our own but something we enter into by grace. In faith, we trust that the Son, our great high priest, "always lives to intercede" for us (Heb. 7:25 NIV). It is only by faith that we can trust that the Spirit prays for us because we do not know how to pray as we ought (Rom. 8:26). Only in faith can we pray knowing that there is "now no condemnation for those who are in Christ Jesus" (Rom. 8:1). Therefore, by faith, we are called out of hiding to pray honestly about the truth in our hearts as those forgiven, redeemed, and reconciled to God through Jesus. We are to come literally in his name—not praying in our names but in the name of Jesus. To understand prayer, we first turn our hearts to the good news of who we are to God, in Christ, by the Spirit.

This means that prayer becomes the first testing ground for the beliefs we affirm. To test our belief that God is the one who forgives, we come out of hiding with the worst of ourselves. To claim that God sees all leads us to present all that is in our hearts and share it with him. This is how we test what Scripture declares to us: "For I am sure that neither death nor life, nor angels nor rulers, nor things present nor things to come, nor powers, nor height nor depth, nor anything else in all creation, will be able to separate us from the love of God in Christ Jesus our Lord" (Rom. 8:38–39). We test this in prayer as we hold our lives open to the God who forgives. "Lord, will you forgive me here? Lord, will this separate me from you?" We must do more than memorize these truths; we have to practice them. Only the experience of knowing our sin in the presence of Christ—and knowing that in him we have forgiveness—will persuade us to be honest and come out of hiding in prayer.

The Good News of Prayer

Of all the benefits received in our salvation, there are two we want to focus on as the "good news of prayer." First, we are the adopted children of the Father, and second, we have been given access to God. We are not called to simply affirm these truths; we must be shaped by them. We need to allow these truths to reshape our life with the Father, to help us grasp what this life of grace, love, and fellowship really is. Doing so opens us up to the good news that we can pray as those forgiven of all our sins.

How do we allow the good news to shape our prayers? By taking a chance on them being true. As we share our most foul thoughts and feelings with our Father in heaven, we walk by faith in his forgiveness, trusting that he will forgive us in these places. If anger is in your heart, come to God as the person who is angry and hold that anger open to him. If lust is in your heart, be the lustful person who needs God's presence, mercy, and healing power. If you realize that you try to use God to get the life you want and your prayer life has become using God rather than being with him, speak that truth to him. He knows. If you discover that you don't want God's presence, tell him and seek him in your unbelief. We put our faith in our adoption by coming as his children who know our only hope is Jesus. Here we know that we are seen, loved, and forgiven, not in our goodness but in our sin.

Our first focus on the good news of prayer is that we have been adopted into God's life. Paul states, "But when the fullness of time had come, God sent forth his Son, born of woman, born under the law, to redeem those who were under the law, so that we might receive adoption as sons. And because you are sons, God has sent the Spirit of his Son into our hearts, crying, 'Abba! Father!' So you are no longer a slave, but a son, and if a son, then an heir through God" (Gal. 4:4–7). We are not merely adopted; we are so united to Christ that his Sonship is now ours. We share in the Son's relationship with the Father. One of the reasons this is important is because of what Paul says next: "God has sent the Spirit of his Son into our hearts crying 'Abba! Father!'"

The Spirit of Jesus cries out, "Abba! Father!" from our depths. But this is not our prayer to pray. Jesus is the one who prays "Abba! Father!" Now that we are his, now that we are united to him by faith, we are caught up into his own prayers. As the Spirit prays, we, too, pray Jesus's prayer to the Father because we are adopted into the Sonship of Jesus (Rom. 8:15). When we pray, we do not come as strangers or as those alienated from the life of God (Eph. 2:19). As the Lord's Prayer teaches us, we pray "our Father" because we pray with the One who prays "my Father" (John 5:18).

The second aspect of the good news might seem less meaningful. In Jesus, we have access to God. That might appear obvious, but it is incredibly important. In Jesus, we are now able to be with God as Father. We have access to the Father because we are one with him who is one with the Father (see John 14:20; 17:22–23). Ephesians 2, likewise, makes this point well:

> For through him [Jesus] we . . . have access in one Spirit to the Father. So then you are no longer strangers and aliens, but you are fellow citizens with the saints and members of the household of God, built on the foundation of the apostles and prophets, Christ Jesus himself being the cornerstone, in whom the whole structure, being joined together, grows into a holy temple in the Lord. In him you also are being built together into a dwelling place for God by the Spirit. (vv. 18–22)

It is *through* Jesus that we have access *to* the Father *in* the Spirit. This is why we pray *to* the Father, *in* the name of the Son, *by* the power of the Spirit. The Father hears us as those who are one with his Son and as those who are his own. He receives us from within the love he has for his Son (John 17:26). Because of Jesus, we have access to the presence of God as his beloved children. This is the space of true prayer, just as the temple was to be a "house of prayer" (Matt. 21:13). In Christ, we are now that house of prayer as we seek his presence. The author of Hebrews encourages us this way:

> Therefore, brothers and sisters, since we have confidence to enter the Most Holy Place by the blood of Jesus, by a new and living way opened for us through the curtain, that is, his body, and since we have a great priest over the house of God, let us draw near to God with a sincere heart and with the full assurance that faith brings, having our hearts sprinkled to cleanse us from a guilty conscience and having our bodies washed with pure water. (Heb. 10:19–22 NIV)

Throughout Scripture, God is said to dwell with his people in the temple. The temple was the place that reminded people of two contrasting things. First, that God was with them, and second, that they didn't have direct access to God. Even though the temple helped people understand that God was with them, it also kept them at a distance. They needed a priest and a sacrifice to mediate for them.

In the book of Hebrews, we discover that this temple framework still remains, but it has changed dramatically. Now we see that the temple building was not the *true* temple, it was only a "shadow" of the true temple. We discover that "Christ has entered, not into holy places made with hands, which are copies of the true things, but into heaven itself, now to appear in the presence of God on our behalf" (Heb. 9:24). Because of this, we "have this as a sure and steadfast anchor of the soul, a hope that enters into the inner place behind the curtain, where Jesus has gone as a forerunner on our behalf, having become a high priest forever after the order of Melchizedek" (Heb. 6:19–20). Our hope resides in another; the anchor of our souls is in heaven.

What If We Don't Want Access?

In response to the reality that Christ has "gone beyond the veil" for us, calling us to himself, we are encouraged to "draw near." In prayer, we are accepting the call to draw near to God and to boldly ascend to his presence in the Son by the Spirit. But if we are honest, God's presence isn't always what we long for. We often long to have God give us his power, healing, forgiveness, and mercy so that we can get on with life. We recognize that God's presence itself can be unnerving and exposing. It can be terrifying to come into the presence of God, and we may unknowingly want to avoid being exposed in his presence. In 1 John 3:19–20, we are told, "By this we shall know that we are of the truth and reassure our heart before him; for whenever our heart condemns us, God is greater than our heart, and he knows everything." Notice that we are "before" God in this example, and our heart is condemning us! This is something we never expected Scripture to say.

I remember reading a book in college about prayer, hoping it would solve my frustrations with prayer. The book was practical, which was good, but in my flesh, I saw that as a way to "fix" my prayer life. I felt guilty for being a spiritual leader and not praying much. So I set out to be better. Instead of drawing near, however, my prayers became ways to come close, but not too close, to God. I wanted a kind of intimacy, but one at arm's length. Like Adam, I was trying to give an impressive speech before God, hoping I could get out of his presence unscathed.

I remember finally recognizing what 1 John 3 was saying and how much encouragement it provided. I know what it is like to have my heart condemn me in God's presence. I know how easy it is to put that on God, as if he were doing it, and then try to find ways to placate him. I know how quickly I turn against myself in these times. But John points us in an entirely different direction. John reminds us that God is greater than our hearts, and he knows everything. God is greater. God knows. Too often our sin and brokenness convince us that the places of our healing and help are dangerous and are the very spaces to avoid. But God is greater. Come *to him*.

For some, many of our seminary students, in fact, prayer has become a place to be harsh on themselves. Somewhere in the hidden recesses of their hearts, they think that if they are vicious toward themselves in God's presence, then God will go easy on them. Rather than coming out of hiding and telling God how angry they are with their spouse or how unsatisfied they are with life, being open to the guilt and shame of these truths, they try to cover them up. Prayer should be a place of freedom, but for these folks it feels more like getting kicked out of school and having to explain it to their mom and dad. When they pray, they are trying to atone for these deep feelings by telling God they are sorry and will never be bad again (deriding themselves for being so bad). How often in our prayers have we sought God's help by promising we'll get our act together?

Notice how idolatrous this kind of praying is, yet how natural it seems. Notice how small a view of God this is. Notice how we can try to transform ourselves apart from the forgiveness and love of Christ. Maybe most painfully, notice how we can cut ourselves off from knowing the forgiveness of God in these places.

Prayer can too easily become a chance to placate God, who we think we can control by being good or hard on ourselves, rather than discovering that in Christ we have access to our Father. Even more so, as the author of Hebrews reminds us,

> Since then we have a great high priest who has passed through the heavens, Jesus, the Son of God, let us hold fast our confession. For we do not have a high priest who is unable to sympathize with our weaknesses, but one who in every respect has been tempted as we are, yet without sin. Let us then with confidence draw near to the throne of grace, that we may receive mercy and find grace to help in time of need. (4:14–16)

The good news of prayer is that God is available and God is your Father. You do not have to remain in solitary confinement in prayer as a way to self-atone. God, who resides in the holiest of heavens, is made available to you in Christ Jesus. As Paul argues in Colossians 3:1–3: "If then you have been raised with Christ, seek the things that are above, where Christ is, seated at the right hand of God. Set your minds on things that are above, not on things that are on earth. For you have died, and your life is hidden with Christ in God." Your life is now hidden with Christ in God. You, as a child of the Father, should seek the things above. You should come to him who calls you his own. Discover that God is greater than your heart, and he knows everything. You have nothing to lose.

But I Don't Know How . . .

Sometimes good news can actually feel like a burden. You get a promotion at work, but now you have *more work*. Sometimes good news seems good on paper, but in practice it is more confusing than before. If we stopped here, we might go to pray and think, *Yes, I don't have to fix myself in God's presence or try to prove my faithfulness. I am a child of the Father, and I can boldly come into his presence in Christ Jesus!* But when we actually pray, we might stop and wonder, *But I still don't know how.* As odd as this might seem, this, too, is good news. In the biblical school of prayer, we need to start with this confession: I do not know how to pray as I ought. Praise God that he knows and has rescued us even here!

The good news is that the Son and the Spirit pray for us. The same God who descended into the very depths of our weakness and confusion, the God who knows we do not know how to pray as we ought, fortunately, knows exactly how to pray for us. We must be reminded that we stand with the apostle Paul, who proclaimed, "In the same way the Spirit also helps our weakness; *for we do not know how to pray as we should*, but the Spirit Himself intercedes for us with groanings too deep for words" (Rom. 8:26 NASB, emphasis added). While it is natural to wonder if we are praying well, the good news isn't that God has given us a secret magic formula for profound prayer. The good news is that the Son and the Spirit pray for us. The same God who descended into the very depths of our weakness and sin, who knows that we do not know how to pray as we ought, understands exactly how to pray for us. God has sanctified space in himself for our prayers, so we draw near in the never-ending love of God.

What makes Paul's claim so amazing is that he tells us we don't know how to pray after Jesus had given the church the Lord's Prayer. Nonetheless, Paul doesn't chastise us, saying, "What do you mean, you don't know how to pray? Didn't Jesus tell you?" Instead, Paul points out that God has done something about it. Scripture does not push us back on our own resources or savvy. Scripture focuses on who God is and what he has done to rescue us. As with 1 John 3, when our hearts condemn us, we are to turn to God in his greatness and goodness and not to ourselves. In our weakness we find help, because the Spirit groans in the depths of our hearts with "groanings too deep for words." Admittedly, that might sound more like weird news than good news. It is better than we may realize.

Imagine you are praying the way you think a good Christian should and are not praying the true desires of your soul. Now imagine God hears your prayers and the Spirit's groaning simultaneously. In one ear God hears your cleaned-up version of prayer, saying the "right" things in the "right" kinds of ways. In the other ear God hears his Spirit groaning in your brokenness, sin, and rebellion. The Spirit groans only in the truth of who you are in light of who you were created to be (Rom. 8:22–23). Think about how your cleaned-up prayers must seem like superficial babbling compared to the deep realism of the Spirit's groans. What an odd sort of clanging your neat and tidy prayers must be against the backdrop of the Spirit's intercession.

Prayer becomes a place to avoid God when we lose sight of this profound truth: We do not create, generate, or perfect prayer. We enter into prayer through the intercessions of the Son and the Spirit for us, through us, and from within us.[1] We turn prayer into a place to avoid God when we think that, even in some small way, it is a place to perform, be good, or appear Christian. That isn't what prayer is. Prayer is trusting in the intercession of Jesus. Prayer is trusting in the Spirit's intercessory groanings. Prayer is entering into their prayers, which means we can speak the truth as the Son and the Spirit speak the truth to the Father on our behalf. This is why we cannot merely learn new prayer techniques; we have to reground ourselves in the good news of prayer. Like in our salvation, we come to prayer with nothing but neediness, sin, and brokenness but find grace, mercy, and steadfast love.

PRACTICE

Prayer beyond Avoidance

Take a moment to consider the ways we described avoiding God in this chapter. Did they resonate with you? If not, take a minute to consider ways you have used prayer to avoid God (e.g., modes of prayer that lead you away from his presence rather than to him, lists of things he can hear and things he cannot hear that guide your prayer, forms of prayer that mirror back accomplishment to you rather than lead you before him). Write them down. Consider these things for only a minute or two, and then turn to prayer. The goal is not merely to know yourself better. The goal is to be with God in truth. So be with him in these things. Ask the Lord, "Father, have I tried to avoid you in my prayer life? What kinds of things do I avoid bringing to you?"

Take five to ten minutes and ask God, "Have I been willing to tell you, God, what I am feeling inside, what I am worrying about, what I am angry about, how I feel toward you, myself, and others in prayer?" Instead of talking to yourself about how angry you are toward others or that you feel like God does not answer your prayers, join the prayers of Christ and the Spirit—tell God about your anger or worry or that you are not sure he wants to answer your prayers. Be honest with your Father. Open your heart to the fact that God knows all and is praying within you. Do not just think these thoughts; pray and see.

Take five more minutes and ask God to show you about those times and seasons of your Christian life when you backed away from prayer. What was going on inside of you that led you to do this? Be open to whatever comes up from your heart. Be open to God in these places.

Finally, consider with the Lord the ways you pray. Ask yourself, *Why have I adopted the methods of prayer I have? Why did*

I choose these and not others? Ask the Lord, "Father, what do I do when something uncomfortable comes up in my heart when I pray? Does that lead me to trust in you and your intercession, or do I feel the need to perform, fix, or control? Father, I have trusted you in my salvation. Help me trust you with my brokenness and continued rebellion."

3

What If Prayer Doesn't Meet My Expectations?

What do you expect God will do when you pray? What do you think God expects of you when you pray? Sometime in my life, I (Kyle) picked up an idea about prayer that no one told me explicitly. I'm not sure I would have been able to recognize it was true of me even if someone had pointed it out. I just didn't have eyes to see it. I expected that prayer was a relationship of exchange, where I would do what I was supposed to do and God would do what he was supposed to do. If I held up my end of the bargain, I was expecting God to uphold his. But we all have different expectations of what that means. What does it mean to pray as we are "supposed to"? What does it mean for God to do what he is "supposed to do"? How do we form these expectations? Prayer was confusing because God didn't meet the expectations I had projected onto him.

Our expectations color a great deal of what we see and hear and, maybe more importantly, how we interpret what our experience means. For the disciples, the expectation that the Messiah would deliver Israel through force made Jesus difficult to understand, especially when he talked about his death, no matter how clear he was about it (Mark 8:31–33). But we have this same problem with others. In our relationships, we discover that we bring a lot of expectations to the table, many of which are unstated or hidden from us. Yet these expectations help form how we think and feel about our relational experiences. We get a compliment from someone but leave with questions in our minds about why or how it was said. We mistake the meaning of a gesture or the lack of a gesture and feel perplexed about an interaction with a loved one. Our boss tells us something in an unexpected tone, and we completely change the meaning of what was said.

When it comes to God, our expectations matter even more. Our assumptions about who he is, who we are in relation to him, and what kinds of things he will and won't do deeply shape our lives with him. These things govern how we judge our faith and, in turn, our life of prayer. Because of this, we must consider who we pray to when we pray, and we need to attend to our expectations in prayer. We have to wrestle with who we believe this God is and what we believe he will be like in order to know what kinds of pray-ers he has called us to be.

Our Father

One of the great gifts of grace is knowing God as Father. But this is a mixed blessing. Notice that God chose a word that, for better or for worse (and it is often a mix), comes with preset expectations. No one uses the word *father* without any assumptions about what it means. For some, a father is someone who is warm and hardworking but relationally unknown and distant. For others, it might mean someone whose wrath spills over at the slightest error and who you must tiptoe around as best you can. For many, a father is someone entirely absent—someone who abandons. For some, a father is someone who satisfies our desires because of his guilt for being away too much (or being too busy to really attend to us). There are, of course, as many possibilities as there are father-child relationships. An important question, therefore, is why God chooses to relate to us through a relationship he knows comes with a lot of baggage.

Maybe more profoundly, God created the parent-child relationship so his redemption would unearth the deepest formation in our lives. God's salvation addresses how we were formed as children in those deep, and often broken, relationships we have with our parents. God doesn't ignore the ways we have been formed, but he awakens the ways we have been loved and broken. This points to a truth about him that we tend not to verbalize. God isn't in the business of destroying and re-creating; he is in the business of redeeming and transforming. This is why the Christian life calls us into our brokenness, sin, and pain and does not simply ignore those things. God calls us to know forgiveness, healing, and redemption in precisely these places. As his children, we need the word *father* healed, no matter how faithful our earthly fathers were. We need to have our understanding of the word re-formed by our heavenly Father.

When we bring the truth of our hearts to God, our response tells us a lot about how we understand what "fathering" is and what our expectations of our fathers are. If we are going to see how this is true in our lives, we have to sit and deeply consider how we actually behave in prayer.

When we are praying and we fall asleep, how do we respond? Is God disappointed in us? Does God expect more from us? How do we respond to a God we believe is disappointed in us? What happens if we find ourselves fantasizing about sinful thoughts in prayer? Or what if prayer has become a place to fight our wandering minds? What does all this mean? What is God calling us to in all of this?

When Prayer Isn't Going Well

Throughout our lives, we have noticed an internal mechanism that has told us whether our prayers were "going well." Perhaps you see this in yourself as well. We judged our prayers negatively if God felt distant, if we were distracted, or if we felt guilty for our lack of fervor. We had certain expectations about prayer, such that if we did our part right, God would feel close. We thought we should have an experience of someone listening, and if we were "praying well," we wouldn't have negative experiences of guilt or shame. But when we did have this experience, we assumed we had done something wrong. Like a child who freezes when dad catches her in disobedience, we would freeze in our prayer and, like that child, try to navigate dad's anger and disappointment.

As I (John) look back on all of this, I see now that I was praying not to my heavenly Father, who sees all and invites me to share all, but to an image of my earthly father (bless his soul). I had come to believe that my earthly father did not really want to hear all my musings or struggles but instead only what was pleasant or good (or at least what was not problematic and messy). I had internalized a notion that what my father wanted was for me to signal that everything was fine—in life and in our relationship—and, therefore, it never dawned on me that God actually wanted to hear what was in my heart. I hadn't seen how my expectations were causing me to misinterpret my experience in prayer. I overlooked that the Son and Spirit were already interceding for me and that my heavenly Father knows what I need before I ask him (Matt. 6:8). I missed that I could tell God anything in the context of his love and forgiveness. I didn't know he wanted to hear me speak the truth about the foulest things in my heart.

But to pray this way, to really enter into deeper, more honest prayer, we have to consider who God truly is. This means we cannot simply memorize the good news of prayer we learned in the last chapter. We have to do more than embrace right information. We have to allow it to shape us, and that takes time. For some of us, the pause button we press in prayer is like a security blanket. It makes us feel safe. It feels good, perhaps, to confess that we've sinned but it feels less so to confess that we're currently sinning. It is more difficult to pray, "Father, I know you hear me, and I trust that you love me, accept me, and have forgiven me, but I have no interest in praying right now. Oh, God, have mercy. Help me!" Honest prayers are difficult.

Prayer Reimagined

I (Kyle) recall the troubling realization of how much my earlier faith was self-serving. I was overcome by how narcissistic my Christian life had been, and how I sought to use God to make my life better rather than abandoning my life to him. In the midst of this, I remember praying, "Lord, I didn't sign up for this." As I looked to the cross, to his call to reject the flesh and my own desperate attempts to create a self in my own power, I knew this was not the reason I put my faith in him. But I had put my faith in him, however naively and simply, and in his grace and mercy, he accepted me. Now I had another opportunity to offer myself to him and trust that he is sufficient. So I meekly prayed Peter's words: "Lord, to whom shall we go? You have the words of eternal life, and we have believed, and have come to know, that you are the Holy One of God" (John 6:68–69). In that moment, my prayer took on the form of that great and honest biblical prayer, "I believe; help my unbelief!" (Mark 9:24). I did believe, and my unbelief became an opportunity to be honest with the Lord.

As we unearth the real desires of our hearts, we begin to see our assumptions about God, and we see more clearly who we really are. In those prayers, we often realize, deep down, that we don't think God wants to hear any of this. These beliefs reveal more our earthly father, perhaps, than our heavenly Father. If God is who he has proclaimed himself to be and ushers us into the prayers of the Son and the Spirit, then there is never a time to hit the pause button in prayer. Trusting in our heavenly Father means we no longer have to accuse or encourage ourselves in prayer. Our hope resides in God and not in our ability to pray properly. Regardless of what we feel, positively or negatively, whether we think God has abandoned us or is closer than ever, we need to bring the full truth to God in humble submission to his grace and mercy. We have no other place to go and no other hope outside of him. God truly is our refuge.

We must learn to banish self-talk from prayer, unless it is a way to give our hearts to the Lord. Proper self-talk in prayer is what the psalmist does, praying, "Why are you cast down, O my soul . . . ?" (Ps. 42:5). The psalmists do not talk to themselves in prayer; they speak to their souls to give the truth to God. God wants to hear what is true of us, and he wants us to share all of our heart with him. When I struggled with questions about whether God was actually present to me, instead of having a debate with myself, I should have brought this to God: "God, where are you? Why do you seem so far away?!" This is the path to real prayer. This will save you from a boring prayer life. This is the place where God's promises become truly known.

One of the real surprises for me (John) was that as I transitioned to deeper honesty in prayer, I realized how little I really believed what I claimed to believe. I believed that Christ died for me in my sins and that I now had access to the Father. But there was much unbelief in me. Only by entering into this unbelief with God did the truth really become internalized into my heart. It takes such an *experience* to know we truly are forgiven all the way through! One of the fruits of God's forgiveness is this kind of honesty in prayer. To believe that God knew all of me led me to pray from this place. This isn't easy though. Praying the truth about what I think God is like terrifies me, worries me, or makes me anxious. But when I began to pray from my unbelief, I started to see what the Lord meant in his teaching on prayer—that we are talking with a new Father, not our earthly one, but our Father who is in heaven.

Now, whenever I pray, I have to tell myself, "John, you are not speaking to your earthly father or any other substitute father. You are speaking to your new Father, who is in heaven. This is your true Father, who sees all, forgives all, and has already experienced the deepest part of you in the prayer ministry of the Spirit [Rom. 8:26] and the intercession of Christ [Heb. 4:13–16]. Therefore, share all in full confidence that he wants to hear what he sees."

Beyond Expectations

For many of us, our expectations about the Christian life were formed early—either in our youth or right after a later conversion. Both of us shared similar expectations, even though Kyle grew up in the church and I became a Christian near the end of high school. We both plunged into an evangelical world full of excitement, optimism, and the deep belief that if things were going well, then we should be elated and experience God's presence. What we discovered is that the history of the church says the exact opposite. We discovered that God meets us in our weaknesses, trials, and failures, even when it seems like he has abandoned us. We came to realize how wrong our assumptions were and how much more profound God's grace is.

Our expectations are most firmly established in our closest relationships. You think you know what your mom and dad will do when you tell them bad news. You believe you know how your spouse will respond to difficulty or good news about your job. Folks see this early in marriage, when they discover a different set of family values, customs, and ways of interaction in their spouse's family. We don't often know how deeply set our expectations are. Many of us don't realize what our family has passed on as "normal" behavior until we are confronted with our spouse's family. We form expectations about how Christmas should go, how birthdays are celebrated, or how to work through (or not work through) relational tension. These expectations do not stay cordoned off in our home; they come to shape our expectations for every relationship. Too often these expectations form how we interpret our life with God without ever being tempered by how God reveals himself.

One clear example of this problem is an implicit assumption about the Christian life. We too often assume our maturity will be a continual defeating of sin, profound growth, and a never-ceasing closeness to God until Christ returns. Few would ever verbalize this. Most of us don't realize we believe it. The problem is that we don't experience it. The longer we are Christians, the more clearly we see our sin. Most of us have experienced long seasons when God seemed distant at best, if not entirely absent, and our joy is sometimes nowhere to be found. At these times it is particularly important to know our expectations. Unfortunately, because our expectations are faulty, we assume the inevitable: *I must have done something wrong. I must not be doing enough. I must not be praying hard enough. I must not be as good as I should be.*

Instead of turning us to God, where our only hope truly resides, our expectations often throw us back on ourselves and our own resources (notice the word *I* in all of those sentences above). Few of us stop to wonder, *Do I have the wrong expectations about the Christian life? Have my assumptions been misguided about what prayer will be?* Interestingly, few of us seem to look to Scripture for this. We are, after all, praying within the prayer life of Jesus and *his* Spirit, and where do we find him? We find Jesus sent by the Spirit into the wilderness to be tempted (Matt. 4:1). We find Jesus praying over and over in the garden of Gethsemane and wrestling through God's calling on his life (Matt. 26:36–46). We find Jesus crying out from the cross to his Father, wondering why God has abandoned him (Mark 15:34). When we experience similar realities, the question shouldn't be, "Why is this happening?" Rather, we need to ask, "Lord, how can I be faithful here?"

In the childhood of our faith, when everything was infused with excitement, zeal, and passion, we were not, unfortunately, filled with knowledge, wisdom, and discernment. In this season of faith, we learned to equate feelings of excitement with God's presence so that they merged into one reality in our hearts. If we weren't excited, we thought we must have done something to chase God away! The arrogance! Even though it was in our sin that Christ died for us (Rom. 5:8), somehow we came to think he was so allergic to it now that he left us whenever we failed to be perfect. We never would have said this out loud. This wasn't an explicit belief for us, and no one ever taught it to us. This was something we came to assume that was only revealed in how we prayed. We see this formation of our hearts by what we think we can and cannot say to God in prayer.

What If This Doesn't Feel Right?

We need to reframe our expectations and remember this: God isn't identical to your feelings, and your feelings do not tell you true things about the world. Your feelings tell you true things about your heart, which is why they are so important. Our feelings and emotions are not adequate signals about the way things are outside of us. We lie to ourselves when we say things like, "She makes me so angry," because what we really mean is, "I am so angry, and she unearthed it in me." It is easier to project our anger onto someone else rather than owning the anger within. With God, we might discover that when we come into his presence, our heart condemns us (as we saw in our discussion of 1 John 3:19–20). When we wrongly assume our feelings tell us true things about reality, we will be tempted to interpret this experience as "God has condemned me." Scripture does not assume our hearts speak truth but rather turns us to truth itself—God, who is "greater than your heart." God has declared who he is to us and calls us to trust in Jesus, our great high priest. Therefore, we should be open to him regardless of what we *feel*. He is greater than these things.

Feelings are like little lights on the dashboard of our souls that tell us, just like the dashboard lights in our car, what is going on "under the hood." Our feelings and emotions reveal to us the deep beliefs and treasures of our hearts, and often, those deep beliefs and treasures explode into our lives unexpectedly. When we drop a dish on the floor and break it, yelling out in frustration, that anger is not created in that moment. The event of dropping the plate merely woke it up. To use a different image, our feelings and emotions are what happen when our soul is punctured. Our emotions leak when we are punctured, which is why they often surprise us. We don't need to choose to be angry at our children; rather, anger flows out. We need to pay attention to this leaking so that we can see the reservoir of pain and brokenness in our souls. We should be watchful of these things in prayer and in life. These signals tell us how our hearts are navigating reality, and in prayer, these signals reveal the heart in the presence of its Lord.

When our hearts condemn us, we shouldn't project this onto God, making him an extension of our feelings. We should discover him as the God of mercy as we wrestle with the lies of our flesh. Feelings of condemnation should create a conversation with God about why we feel condemned and about who we really are in him. This is the real stuff of prayer. To unearth and transform our expectations, we need more than information; we have to live into these realities in our prayer lives. Only by wrestling through these things in prayer do we come to embrace the depths of God's forgiveness, presence, and mercy. It is here where prayer slowly deepens, as water in a stream slowly forms the stones along the contours of the current.

When we come to embrace that God sees and knows, that he searches the deep places of our hearts and calls us to know him as Father in these places, we begin to see how different prayer can be from what we expect. This starts with the good news of prayer we read about in the last chapter. The good news of prayer is that we are forgiven, redeemed, and reconciled to God in Christ Jesus and that we now have him as an advocate before the Father.

By the Spirit we are seen and known and can call God Father. This does not happen all at once, however, but requires a journey into the deep places of our hearts—a journey the Spirit has already taken. As adopted children of God, we must relearn what it means to be a child before a father, but the only way to learn this is to allow our *heavenly* Father to guide what we share with him. Our expectations and prayers will change if we trust that he truly is our Father and that we are his children. This is done in the crucible of sharing all with the One who knows all, prays about all, and forgives all in Christ Jesus, our Lord.

PRACTICE

Praying to a New Father

Take a moment and consider who you pray to. Ask God, "Do I pray to Jesus or the Spirit instead of praying to God as Father? Why?" There are deep questions here, but for our purposes, we should consider how we experience praying to God *as Father*. For some, this is incredibly difficult. The word *father* may come with too much brokenness. If this is true for you, it is understandable why you would come to Jesus rather than to the Father. Nonetheless, over time, you are called to a journey of healing. For others, calling God "Father" is not difficult, but you may never have really grasped how your earthly father formed who you pray to. Take these things to prayer.

Take fifteen minutes and pray the following: "Father, when I come to you, what characteristics do I focus on? Do I see you as distant, angry, uninterested, too busy, or disappointed? Why? Do I see you as soft, warm, and nonjudgmental? Why? How do I understand you, and how has that shaped how I pray?" Be open to seeing how your view of God has shaped your prayers and how this might have undermined what prayer is meant to be. Share this with God. Do not merely consider these sorts of things—bring them to God.

Finally, test your belief that God is the greatest good, full of mercy and forgiveness, and that there is no condemnation for those in Christ Jesus (Rom. 8:1). For five minutes, ask the Father to open your heart to any unresolved feelings you have about him or any reservations you have about his goodness. Ask him to reveal if you wonder whether he really cares for you or has time for your problems or why he feels distant. Share this with him in full candor, exactly as you feel these things, and see where this takes you in prayer. Be open to trusting him with what is in your heart, regardless of whether you deem it good or bad. Trust him and share all, embracing his understanding and forgiveness when needed. In the end, remind yourself that you are in Christ and are forgiven. If this is a joy for you, rejoice. If your heart is still dry as dust, tell God the truth. Ask for grace and mercy in your confusion, and remind your soul that this is why Christ died for you.

If you are doing this reading with others, you might want to write down what happened in prayer and be open to sharing with the group.

4

What If God Wants My Heart of Sin and Pain?

When confronted with sin, failure, or a lack of faithfulness, where do you turn? What do you do when you are confronted by your sin in prayer? As we have seen, in the brokenness of the flesh, we all struggle to believe God is our good Father who wants to hear all we have to share. We struggle to accept the truth that God is our safe harbor and we cannot manage our lives on our own. But this is easier to admit than to live out. In our experience, when struggling with particularly bad or "unclean" sins, we expected our prayers to be met with indignation and rejection until we got our spiritual lives together.

We have seen how our relational experiences with our earthly father shape our expectations about our heavenly Father. Similarly, we all have assumptions about how we are received when we pray. Some think of God rejoicing and welcoming them into his presence. Others, too many I would suspect, believe God rolls his eyes when they come in prayer. Many seem to assume, like the prodigal son did, that they need to present themselves as servants of God since he won't receive them as his children. But unlike the prodigal, who was able to be embraced by his father, we often have a hard time accepting the truth that God loves to flow forth in mercy and that we "are no longer a slave, but a son, and if a son, then an heir through God" (Gal. 4:7).

Notice how different Jonah's assumptions about God are, for instance, compared to the prodigal son's. God told Jonah he was going to punish Jonah's enemies, so you would think Jonah would have been happy about it or even hoped to have a role to play. Yet that is not what we find. Jonah assumed God would be gracious to them even in his condemnation, which is why he rejected God's call. Jonah's governing assumption was that God is gracious and merciful, "slow to anger and abounding in steadfast love, and relenting from disaster" (Jon. 4:2). Unlike us, who sometimes think God is stingy and quick-tempered, Jonah knew God overflows in forgiveness and grace.

Instead of walking into God's call to be formed by mercy and love, Jonah sailed in the opposite direction. When Jonah finally relented, preached to the Ninevites, and watched his worst fears come true, he walked out of the city to pout. Like the father in the prodigal son parable, God also pursued Jonah, revealing to him how broken the loves of his heart really were (Jon. 4:5–11). Our times in prayer will often be the same. In prayer, God invites us to see our brokenness, misguided desire, and unfulfilled longings. We think we are praying about one thing, but the God who is praying within us unveils an entirely different reality about ourselves to know and offer to him. This is why we must hold on to the good news of prayer. Without it, we could not follow where Jesus calls us to go.

We came to realize that our sin had convinced us to flee from the very place God was offering us healing, forgiveness, and love. Like Adam and Eve hiding from God rather than running to him, we thought we needed to manage God rather than reveal all to him. Unfortunately, prayer paid the price. Prayer became more and more unreal and boring, until we hardly ever prayed at all. Not good for theologians! As we began to pray through the real desires and longings of our hearts, something happened. Our prayers began to sound familiar, as if we had a faint recollection of hearing prayers like this before. Our prayers began to sound like the Psalms. Up until this point in our lives, we had avoided the Psalms, especially in seminary, because we couldn't figure out how to study them. We had failed to see that the Psalms are meant to be prayed and are only studied well if they are prayed. Because we did not pray as much as we studied, we weren't able to experience their depths.

Prayer had become a place to be good; therefore, the Psalms seemed like bad prayers.

Praying the Psalms

The Psalms are the church's prayer book, but not because they are first and foremost *our* prayers. Instead, they are the prayers of the people of God that find their fullest meaning in Christ's own praying of them. We now pray these in Christ and in the name of Christ, and in him these prayers can become our own. We are caught up in his praying, and, therefore, Christ's prayers are a training ground to shape our own. This is why we pray the Lord's Prayer and the Psalms—they form our own praying and help us understand what it means to pray to our Father in the name of the Son as fellow children in the Spirit. This means we are called out of ourselves and into the prayers of another, but in doing so, we discover the place, and sometimes the words, that open the truth of our hearts to God.

When we first started praying the Psalms, we both had an odd experience. Over and over again as we prayed, we thought to ourselves, *I can't pray this. God doesn't want me to say these kinds of things. God doesn't want to hear this!* It didn't occur to us at first but soon became obvious that we thought God didn't want to hear, or even *could* hear, his own Word! As crazy as that sounds now, it was evident in how we prayed.

This again raises questions about the assumptions we hold on to and helps reveal ways we limit God, projecting onto him our own presuppositions about what he wants to hear from us. The Psalms help to shape our praying so we can come to the truth of what God can hear. As Dietrich Bonhoeffer says about the Psalms,

> The child learns to speak because the parent speaks to the child. The child learns the language of the parent. So we learn to speak to God because God has spoken and speaks to us. In the language of the Father in heaven God's children learn to speak with God. Repeating God's own words, we begin to pray to God.[1]

In the Psalms, we discover that God really does want to hear. God wants to teach us how to pour out our hearts to him, because our hearts are already open to his gaze (Prov. 15:11). God already sees what is in us—every thought, idea, intention, and struggle of our hearts. He experiences our pain as he groans deep in our souls. God wants us to understand that he already knows our deepest longings, pains, and desires, and through the Psalms, we discover language to give voice to these realities. We have an invitation to pray deeply, and the Psalms serve as the key training ground for that calling.

What Does God See?

We all want to be seen—to truly be looked at and attended to deeply—but we also fear being seen. Like Adam and Eve in the garden hiding from God or a child who runs and hides from her mom and dad because she doesn't want to be seen in her disobedience, the fallen human soul hides in its badness. We want to be seen in our goodness, but when we don't experience goodness, we assume it is better not to be seen.

In the Psalms, we see this tension. On one hand, the psalmist can pray,

> I will rejoice and be glad in your steadfast love,
>> because you have seen my affliction;
>> you have known the distress of my soul. (Ps. 31:7)

For the psalmist, being seen by God was connected to deliverance from evil, and so he can also pray,

> Restore us, O God;
>> let *your face shine*, that we may be saved! (Ps. 80:3,
>> emphasis added)

But there is a shadow side to this desire. What if it doesn't seem like God sees? The psalmist also prays this:

> How long will you hide your face from me? (Ps. 13:1)

> O LORD, why do you cast my soul away?
>> Why do you hide your face from me? (Ps. 88:14)

The psalmist's anxiety about whether God sees leads him to call out to God. The psalmist struggles to understand the brokenness of this world and his own life, in light of God's presence, seeming absence, and guiding providence. Why does it seem that the Lord has turned away?

Notice how the psalmist narrates his own experience and not necessarily reality. Psalm 77:7–8 reflects the heart of a distressed believer in prayer:

> Will the Lord reject forever? . . .
> Has his unfailing love vanished forever? (NIV)

We shouldn't take from this that God has actually turned his face away. We know the experience of the psalmist, and we have shared that experience, no doubt, as Christ himself did. The

Psalms give us permission to pray this prayer as a reflection of our own wrestling with God.

Similarly, when confronted with sin and our own struggle with faithfulness, we might get to a place where God's sight is unnerving and so we pray,

> Turn your gaze away from me, that I may smile again,
> before I depart and am no more. (Ps. 39:13 NRSV)

In these moments, we pray the truth of our hearts but realize God has a better way.

Perhaps the most deceptive temptation is to believe that the way we see ourselves is the way God perceives us. This is deceptive because it takes our own brokenness and projects it onto God. When we pray, "Why do you hide your face from me?" which is a perfectly good and honest prayer, what we really should mean is, "Lord, why does it feel like you are hiding your face from me?" What we shouldn't assume is that our feelings are telling us true things about reality—and particularly about God. Deep down, many of us believe that if it feels like God is absent, then he is absent. We fail to recognize that we live in the age of faith, and not the age of sight, which is the age to come (1 Cor. 13:12). Because of this, prayer invites us into struggle with God—to tell him why we are struggling with him. Rather than seeing those struggles as invitations into a deeper life of prayer, we are tempted to just "pray better."

When we grit our teeth and pray better, we tend to turn to fantasy. Our Father in heaven calls us to himself in his Son by the Spirit to unearth the truth. He calls us into his presence in reality and not fantasy. But we seek fantasy because it feels safer, and we think that maybe God won't notice. Sometimes this feels safe because we fantasize about having God on our own terms or we compare our lives with those who we think are less faithful (or just more sinful!) than we are. Sometimes our fantasies scare us, like when we worry God is who we deeply fear him to be—unforgiving, impatient, and ruthless. This fantasy also feels safe for some because it affirms the deepest fears of the heart. It feels familiar. This can also feel safe because it provides a path to deal with our fear in our own power. We think, *If God is unforgiving and impatient, then I have to be better.* Prayer once again becomes a place to be good, and we cease being honest. This is particularly evident when we discover extremely negative emotions in prayer.

When confronted with these negative emotions, we are tempted to short-circuit prayer to do what God is supposed to do. "Perfect love casts out fear," John tells us in 1 John 4:18. But in our fear, anxiety, guilt, and shame, we don't turn to our Father, who is perfect love, but instead we seek to take care of these negative emotions ourselves. The *idea* of perfect love doesn't cast out fear; only perfect love himself can do that. By our trying to clean ourselves up and do the work that God alone can do, prayer is put in service of our need to feel good about our spiritual life. If we go to prayer looking for a mirror to reflect our goodness back to us, prayer will never be a life-giving place of honesty. As we have seen, this is why prayer is often alienating, lonely, and, quite honestly, boring. When this happens, it means prayer has become a place to manage God—and that will never fuel an intimate life of prayer.

But God, I'm So Angry

My (John's) anger helped me see how upside down my prayers had become. While talking to God, I noticed some deep anger, or at times resentment and pain, in my heart. I had a knee-jerk reaction, which would again cause me to press the pause button on prayer and begin talking to myself. This became my way of turning to self-management instead of to God. My anger felt wrong, and my pain made me feel weak. Instead of bringing these feelings to God, I would pause prayer and say to myself, "John, it is not good to be angry. It doesn't help. The anger of man does not achieve the righteousness of God, so let it go." I would not address my pain, not even to myself. Then I would unpause my prayer and say, "Sorry, God, I should not be so angry at this person. Forgive me." Then I would try to continue praying.

Notice that my goal was to move past my pain and resulting anger rather than actually dealing with them—or more important, letting God deal with them within me. Rather than seeing my pain and anger in reality, I turned to fantasy, thinking I could just speak them away. This well-intentioned act of self-management, however, has no power to deal with deep-seated anger. It merely stuffs the anger down, leaving it untouched and ready to spring up again. Moreover, and this is the point: this kind of self-talk is about me doing all the work of cleaning myself up by self-management. Why am I tempted to do this? Because I want to think of myself as a good Christian, a strong Christian, one who is beyond nursing pains and anger.

Because I don't want to see who I really am inside, I hide and cover up like Adam and Eve. Now, "being good in prayer" is my hiding and covering. But our Father in heaven sees all, knows all, forgives all, and wants to hear all. God wants to transform all the pain and brokenness in the hearts of his children. You and I may need to reread that sentence! Our temptation, unfortunately, does not go away easily, because it is the continued echo of the first sin in all of our hearts. Since the first sin, we've believed that we can be like God. In prayer, being "like God" is trying to address our sin, pain, and brokenness on our own.

Instead of fixing my sin and learning to manage my anger, fears, and anxieties, I must come to God. It is only in my abiding in him that these will cease to dominate my life and define my inner world. Only God can clean me up and deal with my anger. I must come to him to discover Christ in full forgiveness and love so I can walk in the Spirit in his transforming work. To walk in the Spirit and relearn what my anger is about with the Spirit, I have to embrace what my anger is doing within me and what God wants to do with it. I must attend to what he wants to teach me about my anger;

therefore, I have to come to God in the reality of my life and share that anger with him.

We will explicitly address how to pray our anger Paul-style (and Psalm-like) in part 2, but for now it is helpful to reflect on what you truly think God can hear.

Do you bring your fears, anxieties, anger, struggles, and brokenness to God in prayer, or are there key things you leave out?

What do you do when, like the psalmist, you feel God has turned his face away?

Do you call out to him and seek his face, or do you turn to self-management to try to fix what you think is the problem?

Praying in Reality

This, in many ways, brings us back full circle to consider where our hope truly resides. When we are confronted with the truth of ourselves, where do we turn? When we read something in Scripture that rebukes something in our hearts, whether that is sin, anxiety, or even the sense that God is absent, where do we go? How do we navigate these struggles? Scripture is a two-edged sword that cuts us to the deepest part of our being, exposing the "thoughts and intentions of the heart" and leaving us "naked and exposed" before God (Heb. 4:12–13). What do we do in that place?

We must grapple with this astonishing truth: God can hear what he sees. More to the point for our purposes, what God sees he wants us to pray. Whatever is in our hearts—hidden sins, deep and unmet longings, pains, and sorrows long left hidden—are what God is calling us to pray. The Spirit is lifting these to the Father in his groaning. When we avoid naming the truth in prayer, we are praying from outside of the Spirit's groaning. God wants to hear what he sees because he is always at work in reality and never in fantasy. This is the fruit of the good news of prayer.

When the Word leaves us naked and exposed, with the thoughts and intensions of our hearts truly seen, the author of Hebrews reminds us that "we have a great high priest who has ascended into heaven, Jesus the Son of God" (Heb. 4:14 NIV). Because of this, we can "approach God's throne of grace with confidence, so that we may receive mercy and find grace to help us in our time of need" (v. 16 NIV). Scripture does not send you back on yourself when convicted. God does not push us to rely on our savvy to manage or fix or muster other strategies to make ourselves safe in his presence. There is no hope in that. We have a great high priest, so we must set our hope on him.

Jonah was right—God is gracious and merciful, slow to anger and abounding in steadfast love (Jon. 4:2). When our sin and brokenness are exposed, especially in prayer, we have only one place to go: God. Since we have a great high priest in Jesus, who has ascended into heaven, into the very presence of the Father, we can now approach God's throne of grace in confidence even with our hearts fully exposed. In faith, we do not approach the throne in our name but in the name of Jesus. In faith, we know that by his wounds we have been healed (1 Pet. 2:24) and in his word we have been made clean (John 15:3). We are now children of the Father.

The work of salvation that God has done in Christ creates the context for prayer to become real. *What he sees, we are invited to share*—to approach the throne of grace with confidence. This is the only way to finally find freedom, to enact the freedom we have in Christ by sharing all that is in our hearts. This is true for all our thoughts but maybe especially for the foulest of them. Only then will we be convinced that God is for us and that nothing "will be able to separate us from the love of God in Christ Jesus our Lord" (Rom. 8:39).

Once we begin to pray what God truly sees, we are praying in the reality of faith. As we pray the foulest things in our souls, we begin to grasp how far-reaching God's forgiveness and the cross truly are. Christ's work reaches to the deepest places of our faithlessness, brokenness, and sin. We can fully come to grasp what Paul said to Timothy in 2 Timothy 2:13, that even "if we are faithless, he remains faithful—for he cannot deny himself" (and his covenant with the Father on our behalf). We begin to know, not just abstractly but *in experience*, that nothing can separate us from the love of God in Christ Jesus. Moreover, we begin to see that *we* are loved even as we experience the filthiest place in ourselves with Him. Coming to know that we are loved—not in our good character but in Christ—is the basis of the prayers in the Psalms.

This is why praying the Psalms can be so difficult. Most of us are not used to this level of honesty with ourselves, let alone with God! When we come across vengeance against one's enemies in the Psalms, it is easier to pretend like we don't have this kind of anger and that we should not feel this way as a believer, regardless of what our social media feeds, freeway driving, or family might say about us. Instead, we should wrestle with our own anger when we pray through the hate found in Psalm 139, proclaiming,

> I hate them with complete hatred;
> I count them my enemies. (v. 22)

Do you truly hate someone? Are you aware of the anger residing within you? Or do you deny it or confess it quickly or look for excuses when it comes out (like when you are cut off on the highway, when your kids disobey you, when life simply doesn't seem to work, or when you talk politics)?

Psalm 139 should lead us into the truth of our anger, making us acknowledge that since God sees all, we must share all, even if that leads us to pray that God would kill someone and take vengeance! As we pray these truths of our hearts, we should be led, as the psalmist was, to honestly ask God to search our hearts and see if there is any offensive way in us (Ps. 139:23–24). As we admit the anger, rage, and perhaps hatred in our hearts, we put this in the hands of our great high priest, trusting that he is the true judge.

Love Your Enemies and Pray

When we think about bringing our anger to God, we probably begin worrying about Jesus's words in Matthew 5:43–45: "You have heard that it was said, 'You shall love your neighbor and hate your enemy.' But I say to you, Love your enemies and pray for those who persecute you, so that you may be sons of your Father who is in heaven." When we read this, we can imagine that what Jesus wants from us is to try hard not to be angry. But notice that Jesus still assumes you can name your enemy. He doesn't say, "Imagine a scenario when you were still angry and still had enemies." Jesus assumes you have both anger and enemies. In prayer we must name the truth of these things, but naming them is not enough. We do not simply name our anger and move on. We name our anger in the presence of Christ, the One who loved us even when we were his enemy.

When that person who drives us crazy awakens anger deep within us, we need to bring the truth before God, who has forgiven the deepest sins in our hearts. Honesty is fundamental for living in the kingdom of God. We need to name truth, to live in the reality of our hearts, and to be honest about the truth of who we are. But none of these things are the goal. We bring the truth of ourselves to God in light of his proclamation about his kingdom, praying that he will take us on a journey from hatred to enemy love. In our anger, when confronted with our enemies, we need to name the truth of our hearts and reframe it with the reality of God's kingdom.

Importantly, naming our anger does not justify it. Naming what is true helps us come to him who calls us to a better way—to love, forgive, and pray for our enemies. In his grace, he receives us as we are; and in his grace, he refuses to leave us there. The first place to wrestle through these things is in prayer. Some of our students struggle with honesty in prayer because it feels faithless to talk with God about their sin and brokenness. God's holiness makes them nervous. They assume he wants them to condemn their sin and brokenness and move on, spending as little time as possible thinking about these kinds of things. But honesty about sin and brokenness is not justifying them or somehow accepting them as good. The opposite is true. Ignoring these things or condemning our sin and moving on is a failure to take them seriously. Honesty in prayer is not having a lax view of sin. Honesty in prayer is a rejection of dishonesty, or a lack of transparency, in prayer. The opposite of honesty in prayer is sending our "good Christian" avatar to pray instead of coming to God ourselves.

As we follow this path of prayer, the Spirit uses the truth to teach us that we have nothing to fear. Until we pray what God sees in us, we will not really know who God is and what he can hear and handle, because our anxiety and fear will inhibit our knowledge of God and ourselves. This leads to a double delusion. On the one hand, we foolishly believe God doesn't really see, and on the other, we believe that what he does see he doesn't want to hear about. The result is the naive thinking that if we avoid telling God about the deep issues in our hearts, they will just go away or can be dealt with over time. This has led too many to believe that these things don't reside in their hearts any longer. This leads to worship, prayer, and seeking Jesus in fantasy rather than living by faith in reality. When we abide by this double delusion, we introduce a ceiling on our trust in God.

Contrary to this, when we trust that God is who he says he is—that he is full of grace and mercy and he wants to hear what he sees—we discover how honesty leads us deeper and deeper into his embrace. Now I can read the Word and see the truth that I am anxious, fearful, and, at times, angry. Instead of turning to my own ability to fix these broken aspects of my life (an ability I don't have), the good news is that I desperately need God, and he has given himself to me in Christ Jesus by the Spirit. I can let the Word lay bare my thoughts, split open my heart and conscience, and take me into deeper and more honest conversations in love.

I don't have to be afraid of the truth of who I really am, because Christ died for me in reality and calls me to abide in him where I really am.

Prayer As If Grace Were Real

For some, this all seems counterproductive. They think, *I just need to stop acting out in my anger or stop worrying or get over my pain. And I need to put my sins in the past.* This is the common sense that Scripture calls the flesh or, sometimes, "self-made religion" (Col. 2:23). This is seeking to depend on our own power against our sin. But consider who Jesus attended to in his ministry—people whose sins, pains, and brokenness were on the surface. It was the man who cried out to God in the temple, who "beat his breast, saying, 'God, be merciful to me, a sinner!'" (Luke 18:13) who left justified, not the Pharisee who sought to pray in his goodness. Jesus did not embrace the Pharisee who invited him for dinner but received the woman who awkwardly wet his feet with her tears (Luke 7:36–50). Jesus's words to the Pharisees are important to recall: "He who is forgiven little, loves little" (Luke 7:47). This is why we needn't be afraid of seeing the truth of our hearts. The more we see our need for forgiveness the more we can come to know we are forgiven, which Jesus links to our ability to love. Our call is to love and to walk deeper into love, and thus we need to embrace all the things for which we have been forgiven.

Prayer is a journey into our pain and sin, because faith is a journey with God in truth. It is in our pain, and in the pangs of conscience regarding our sin, that we are crying out to know, *Am I really forgiven here? Is healing available for me in these places? Can God truly receive me here?* We are called to trust that as we see our sin and brokenness, we are confronted with an invitation into love and forgiveness. Here we come to see and to know how profoundly deep, intimate, and freeing this love of God truly is. This means that our journey into love is a journey into how deeply we need forgiving. Unlike the expectations of my young Christian life, this is not a journey defeating sin in my strength and growing in independence. Our journey is grasping ever more tightly on to the truth that without Christ we can do nothing and entering into deeper realizations about our brokenness and sin. We don't need to be afraid of what we find in our hearts; this is now the pathway of embracing the forgiving grace and mercy of God.

PRACTICE

Praying My Sin and Pain

For ten to fifteen minutes, talk to the Lord and speak to your soul (as in the Psalms) about what you have tended to do in prayer with your sin, pain, guilt, and feelings of shame. Ask the Lord, "Do my pain, sin, and feelings of failure have a place in my prayers? Am I able to share these things with you?" Ask the Lord whether you secretly hope God will heal your pain like he heals limbs and eyes in Scripture. Do you pray, "Lord, make this go away" without really being present to it or sharing the fullness of it with the God who sees? Consider areas of your life where you feel pain, whether it has to do with disappointment about family troubles and friction, with a job or another life situation, or with a relationship in which you have been treated poorly. Take this into prayer. Let the Spirit be with you, and allow yourself to relearn how to walk with him in these feelings.

"Father, you know and you see. You see my anger, frustration, and regret." Take a few minutes to share with the Lord your responses to the pains in your life, regardless of what they are. Maybe you have sought revenge. Maybe you have allowed hatred to well up deep within you. Take that to him. Bring him your worries and fears. Invite him into your pains. Instead of managing your emotions, bring them to God and relearn what it means to experience pain in the Spirit. This is the beginning of relearning how to walk in the Spirit, particularly in the disordered, hurt, angry, and sinful areas of your heart.

INTERLUDE

An Invitation to Relearn Prayer the Lord's Way

Whenever a worship leader introduces a new song, I (Kyle) sigh a bit in my heart. I find new songs frustrating because I cannot yet praise God with them. I spend the whole song trying to figure out how to sing, causing me to think more about the song than the God I am supposedly singing to. It takes me a while to conform with the melody, understand what the words are saying, and then make the words, in some sense, my own before I can really use it as a vehicle to present myself to God.

I have a similar problem with church services. I first need to catch the overall contours of a service before I really grasp its rhythm. Jonathan Edwards used to say that the Christian life is learning a new song we will sing for eternity. Now we are discordant notes in the grand symphony of praise taking place in heaven, but in the spirit of the great hymn "Come, Thou Fount of Every Blessing," the Lord is tuning our hearts to sing his grace. We are all learning a new song, a song whose melody, lyrics, and overall rhythm we are struggling to make our own.

Internalizing new songs takes time. Singing another's words forms us, for better or worse, for our own praise of God. Prayer is no different. One might think, from what we've said thus far, that the only honest prayer is praying whatever comes up from one's heart. But this would neglect that there is a training ground for prayer, just as worship songs are meant to train our extemporaneous praise. When we take on the biblical training of prayer, we are called to step into prayers that are not our own. These prayers help shape our praying. This may feel foreign, odd, and maybe even inauthentic. We don't tend to value this form of apprenticeship much anymore. Culturally, we appreciate originality more than imitation, but there is something deeply broken about that.

When Jesus's disciples asked him to teach them to pray, he gave them a set prayer, what we call the "Lord's Prayer." As we have already seen, the prayer book of the Bible is 150 set prayers, by which we are called to step into the prayers of another, wrestling through what it means to allow these words to become our own. This is an invitation to learn a new song that will shape all of our singing. But this training is not mere repetition. By taking on another's words, we open our hearts to learn the rhythm, movement, and lyrics of a song we are being formed to sing. If we discover that our hearts are out of tune with the reality of God and his kingdom, all kinds of pain, confusion, or boredom may result. We will need to be honest if we are going to abide in the Lord's work to tune our hearts in to his grace.

Transformed Prayer

Our experience of prayer is often like a house of mirrors, reflecting our hearts back to us in all sorts of broken and inaccurate ways. We can pray for decades without recognizing how those mirrors are blinding us to the truth. We need to recognize how our prayers can be our way of trying to manipulate God, attempting to say the right words in the right order as if we were reciting a magical spell, or simply using prayer as a tool to secure God to our side. Prayers can be messy. For those of us who grew up in the church, or who have been Christians for a long time, prayer can also be so "normal" that we don't even pay attention to how we pray. We just do it (or don't). Familiarity can blind us to what we are doing in prayer or what is happening in our praying that we are barely aware of. This can lead us to avoid prayer because we might not know what we are supposed to be doing in the first place. Prayer is one of the most fundamental practices of the Christian but also one of the least explored in the Christian community. Like sex, prayer is a topic few people seem to want to talk about openly, yet it profoundly shapes our lives.

It is not surprising that the disciples asked Jesus to teach them how to pray. Prayer raises many questions. The disciples, of course, knew *something* about prayer. They had prayed and heard the Psalms, and they had prayed in the temple. Seeing Jesus praying spurred them to ask for help. Luke tells us that "Jesus was praying in a certain place, and when he finished, one of his disciples said to him, 'Lord, teach us to pray, as John taught his disciples'" (Luke 11:1). The disciples were asking two things from their teacher: First, "How do *you* pray, Jesus?" and second, "How does your teaching guide our praying?" Jesus did not immediately launch into how-to questions about prayer but began naming the deeper motives that beguile our Christian lives. He had already excavated the deepest motivations of the heart as the real issue concerning sin and raised concerns about what it means to come into the presence of a holy God (Matt. 5:1–6:8). It is no wonder they asked about prayer after they heard him say,

> You have heard that it was said, "You shall not commit adultery." But I say to you that everyone who looks at a woman with lustful intent has already committed adultery with her in his heart. If your right eye causes you to sin, tear it out and throw it away. For it is better that you lose one of your members than that your whole body be thrown into hell. And if your right hand causes you to sin, cut it off and throw it away. For it is better that you lose one of your members than that your whole body go into hell. (Matt. 5:27–30)

Jesus's teaching was a mirror to show the disciples there was no place to hide from their sin so he could prepare them to hear the good news. He revealed how prayer can become a place to impress others (Matt. 6:5) and then called them to pray in secret. Jesus addressed his disciples' temptation to impress themselves and others with their spiritual savvy and highlighted their temptation to pray in a way that sought to ensure God would hear. Do not be like the Gentiles, we are told, who think their many words will make them heard (Matt. 6:7–8). We do not need to say many words to cajole God to listen. Rather, Jesus unveils a deep truth: *God can be approached as a Father who knows what we need even before we ask.*

The message to us is this: God knows what you need before you even put your prayer into words. Don't be troubled because you stumble over your words, and don't worry if you are not passionate enough or sincere enough. He is your Father, so come to him. He already knows what you need before you do. If, like Martha, your heart is worried and anxious about many things and the worry and fear spill over in prayer, then come as the one who worries and is anxious. New Testament scholar Craig Keener, referring to Paul's command not to be anxious (Phil. 4:6), claims, "Paul's alternative to worry is not the anxious attempt to suppress it but rather acknowledging the needs to God and entrusting them to him."[1] This is exactly right.

It is precisely at this place where prayer feels so odd. The notion that prayer is intimate and honest is not difficult to understand even if it is difficult to practice. But if prayer is such a profoundly intimate place, then why does Jesus give us a set prayer? It may feel like it undermines the intimacy, like reading old novels and hearing a wife refer to her husband as "Mr. Edwards." It is this kind of formalism that pushes against our sensibilities. It's interesting, however, that no one has taken Jesus's teaching on the Lord's Prayer to mean that we are only supposed to pray this exact prayer. Or that he gave it to us so we never have to pray on our own. No one has ever come to the conclusion that Jesus was providing the one prayer Christians are allowed to pray or somehow a set equation for "getting prayer right."

In this sense, the Lord's Prayer has a similar role to what the temple system had for Israel. This system included all sorts of regulations about being near God, such as cleansings, sacrifices, and offerings, and followed a rhythm of special days, special services, and special meals. But it was never *about* these things. The goal was to form the people of God for life *with* God, not to form them for the rituals themselves. Too often God's people mistook the rituals as ways to manage him rather than as means for communing with him. Too often God's people focus on the form and miss the purpose. Too often we concentrate on getting the song right but fail to use it to come to the Lord. We can make the same mistake with the Lord's Prayer.

The Conditioning Prayer

In the Lord's Prayer, we discover that Jesus does, in fact, provide us a way to pray. It is not, importantly, a way to manipulate God. Rather, this prayer is the way to enter into reality. It is a conditioning prayer. In other words, this prayer conditions and forms how we approach God as his children. It guides and shapes all of our praying, conditioning our prayers according to what is truly real. To pray this prayer is to step into the words, and even the world, of another—of Jesus, who forms our hearts to pray these words truly.

By praying the words *our Father*, we recognize that we pray with Jesus, who prays *my Father*. By praying to our Father, we recognize the grace we have been given in Christ Jesus. I am a child of the Father within the Sonship of Jesus, so I pray from within the relationship he has with the Father. Jesus is the one who prayed this prayer truly. His life is the life lived in harmony with this prayer. This is not simply a form prayer; it establishes the movement of how a child prays to their Father. It *is* Jesus's prayer, now available to sinners who are adopted into God's family through Christ's intercession.

As Jesus's prayer, the Lord's Prayer acts as a mirror for our own praying to God. The Lord's Prayer is a training ground that re-forms our prayers by leading us in words that are not our own. This prayer conditions our prayers by refocusing us on who God is, who we are, and what life in the kingdom is like. Jesus's words help us understand what it is to have a real conversation that breaks through the fantasy and fear and into what is most real. Jesus is teaching us to converse with our Father in heaven—how we can grow from our infantile fantasies of wanting God on our terms—to embrace the truth about what God is doing in the world and even in our own prayers.

Our Father in Heaven

To pray *our Father* is to step into the status and identity of another. I am a child of the Father. The second I utter the word *Father*, I know that I am called to know God on his terms and not mine. God calls us to use a word he knows has baggage. As we have seen, for most of us, a mix of things are associated with the word *father*. For some, a lot of brokenness is wrapped up in that word. Therefore, right away, this prayer forces us to ask some questions about what this word means when we say it.

In light of our Father in heaven, you might ask how you talk to your "father on earth." You are already conditioned to speak to your father. Your relationship with your earthly father has already shaped you, in part, and therefore formed your heart in ways you do not see. But now you stand before a new Father. Your Father in heaven, who already knows your heart, is not afraid and wants you to share your heart with him.

It is important to pause here. God knows your heart and all you need before you ask. This should lead you to wonder, *How would I have talked to my earthly father if I had known he already knew what was in my heart yet received me with open arms anyway?* In doing so, you may recognize that the ways you tried to manipulate your earthly father are the same ways you try to manipulate God in prayer. You may realize that your expectations about your father's presence have conditioned your expectations with God. Whatever you bring in prayer that has been conditioned by your earthly father is meant to be transformed by your heavenly one.

By standing before *our* Father and not merely *my* Father, we must embody a further realization. God does not simply love us, he loves the world (John 3:16). That is, God loves those who we don't. He loves and cares deeply about his world in ways we don't. This conditions our petition about others we are struggling with. We may want them to change, repent, or meet our needs—and this may be motivated not by love but by guilt, anger, or wanting a hassle to end. But God is just as much their Father. We have to be honest about how our loves do not match the loves of the Lord. This Father we pray to is the God of all things, the Creator, the one from whom all creation comes and depends on and the one who looks down from heaven and can do what he desires. Prayer is the space where we must come to realize that our desires may not mesh with his.

As we pray the Lord's Prayer, we must wrestle with the truth that our desires are in need of transformation. Perhaps our petitions need transformation. We must bring them in truth, because to deny them would be to live in fantasy. That is always a temptation. Regarding our own struggles, it is easy to think, *God says not to be anxious, so stop it. Stop being anxious and get it together.* This kind of self-talk fails to embrace God in truth, and, in this example, will probably only raise anxiety rather than quench it. Turning to the Lord's Prayer in these places is not mastering a technique to make sure God will answer. Rather, the Lord's Prayer leads us in our anxiety to the God we know as Father and before whom we are known as his children.

Recall the parable of the father with two sons, often called the parable of the prodigal son (Luke 15:11–32). One of the most glaring points of the parable, but one we can easily miss, is that the older brother—the one who was "good," stayed home with his father, and did what he was told—ended up looking nothing like his father. His father pursued both his sons in love, but the older son rejected his younger brother and refused to go with his father. The older son, like the younger one, came to see his relationship with his father in primarily economic terms, and so failed to see the treasure he had was life *with* the father.

When the father sought his oldest son to share in the generosity he was lavishing on his youngest, his son barked at him, "Look! These many years I have worked like a slave for you, and I never disobeyed your commands" (Luke 15:29 NET) and went on to call his brother "this son of yours" (Luke 15:30). The older son had learned to play the role of a son but not embody the reality of a son before his father. The Lord's Prayer mirrors these realities in our hearts to shepherd us into the truth. It helps us see ways we are not like our Father in heaven. It helps us see how our praying may be attempts to woo God to our side, to prove we are good, or to simply use God to rid ourselves of guilt. If we are watchful, we see that this is a failure to pray as a child of our heavenly Father. To pray as a child entails naming the truth of our hearts in prayer, whatever that truth is. We are to recognize God is a new kind of Father—the perfect Father—and have that shape our hearts.

The two great temptations in God's presence are polar opposites, but they lead to the same place. The first temptation is believing that God desires for us to clean ourselves up and project whatever goodness at him we think he wants to see. This is typically understood as the "Pharisaic temptation," which is an attempt to present our whitewashed exterior to God while trying to hide the dead bones of our souls. This leads to prayerlessness or a kind of praying in which we seek to manage ourselves and

God to feel "okay" about ourselves. This praying will never fuel a deep life with God.

The second temptation is to think that because God is love, he does not call us to be conformed to his life. This kind of God is less about holiness and justice and more about pure acceptance, like the Father who does not care what we do but simply wants a hug at the end of the day. So instead of bringing our brokenness and sin to God, recognizing that we need to address both, we get rid of the idea of sin and talk only about brokenness. This, too, leads to a kind of prayerlessness, because God becomes a mirror to affirm our hurt, autonomy, and worldliness and, therefore, a tool to reflect the person we want to be. Both temptations focus on how we can use God to gain the life we want. In both we make the mistake of keeping ourselves in the center rather than finding our lives "hidden with Christ in God" (Col. 3:3), where he is the center of life and we need to be conformed to him. Both fail to see how good the good news of prayer really is.

Conformed to Reality

As we pray the Lord's Prayer, we place ourselves in reality. This is a prayer of faith and hope, where we seek to have faith and hope in what we are praying, even as we recognize ways that our lives may not conform with these words in full. First and foremost, this prayer calls us to be children before the Father. Yet, as we enter into the body of the prayer, we come across six commands. These are not the sorts of commands that should be heard as "You, God, go do this!" Rather, these are commands we internalize as ways to name our intention. To pray these commands in faith and hope is to intend that they be true of us. This is to do what God asks of us in Proverbs, to "incline your ear to my understanding" (Prov. 5:1). So what does this prayer have us intend?

To pray, "Let your name be holy" is to intend that God's name be holy and lifted up in all we pray and do. As we ask that our mother be healed of her cancer or that our cousin come to know Christ, we need to do so in the reality that God is to be known as holy in all situations. Even if we do not feel or even really grasp this, we are accepting the invitation to enter into this truth. As we pray for our mother or cousin, we are asking the Lord to reveal how his being holy can condition our prayer. We are holding open our desire to see how his holiness can be realized or made more apparent in the situations of our lives. But now we are confronted: Do we really care about God or his holiness in all of this, or do we just care that our mother be healed?

We must not hide here. We must be open to the truth in this place of prayer. We need to be open to how the Lord's Prayer confronts us, and as we pray for God's holiness to be known, we watch and see how this squares with our real desires. If it does, wonderful. We are growing into what is real. If our hearts aren't interested in God's holiness, it is important that we see and know this—and use it to turn to the God of mercy. This should not take our attention away from prayer but should instead now form how we pray.

The second intention made in the Lord's Prayer is this: "God, in all I ask of you, let your kingdom come. That is what I hope in this prayer. This is my intent in asking you." As we pray for the salvation of a friend or our personal financial situation, the reality is that God already knows what we need and knows what is best. He is not waiting for our directions or instructions; he is calling us to open our needs to him in light of his kingdom being realized in my life. So maybe we pray, "Father, you know I want a raise in my salary. May your reign be manifest in this and your ways be realized in my life. Let Jesus, the King of all, rule over this request and what I need. If you plan to fulfill this now, or if you are calling me elsewhere in this, may your will be done."

Once again, the mirror is set before us. Ask yourself, "Do I really care about Jesus being manifested in my request, or do I only care about getting what I want? How does the economy of Jesus's kingdom contrast with or relate to my prayers?" We have prayed many "good" requests to God that were more conditioned by our understanding of how the world should work or how our wants and desires work than by "your kingdom come." We should still make those requests, but we must hold them before God in the truth of our intentions. We have nothing to lose in our honesty with God but much to lose in our hiddenness.

The third intention influences all that we talk to God about: "Father, as I ask for this healing, for going to this graduate school, or for who I would marry, I hope your will to be done in my life. I hold these desires before you, asking that your will would be done on earth, just as in heaven." Once again, the mirror of reality is presented. Do we really want God's will if it contradicts what we will? Are we interested in God's will, or do we see God as the way to get our own will done? Most of us genuinely have a desire for God's will to be done—regardless of the outcome—but we also want our desires fulfilled no matter the cost. As we attend to this truth in ourselves, we go to God, saying, "Father, have mercy; here I am. God, you know what is best. I am your servant. Even if I don't really want your will but my own, thank you for forgiving me and for your patient love for me. In the Spirit, I rejoice in the thought of your will being done, even as a corrective to my own, but help me in my flesh as I long to have my way instead of yours."

Reordering Our Reality

As our prayers are being conditioned according to God's holy name, his kingdom reign, and his will being done on earth as it is in heaven, we also turn to the next three conditioning intentions. In all our requests to God, we seek to name not only the truth of God's will but also the reality that our self-centered lives must be re-centered around God and others. When we pray *our* Father, it is true that we pray this with Jesus, who can pray *my* Father, but it is also true that we pray this with the communion of saints. We pray with others, as we are members of others.

This second set of three intentions helps us remember our status as children. We are not in command. We are not called to assert our wills against the world. Therefore, our requests need to be transformed by the presence of a superior into humble petitions and requests. We can pray, "God, if you would be pleased in so doing, give us . . . forgive us, as we forgive . . . lead us . . . deliver us. . . ." In doing so, we are reminded that our personal prayers are requests for *us*. We are not alone in the need for these things. When we pray as children of the Father, we do not pray alone, but other people condition our prayers. Praying as a child is always praying as a brother or sister of these numerous other children of the Father, fellow children with needs and desires like our own (and often greater than our own). In all we pray, our requests must be shaped by these intentions.

The first petition is for God to give us what we need for our daily sustenance. Here we are challenged to evaluate all that we ask and to consider whether we are really open to God to give us what is needed for this day. Ask yourself, "Do I trust that the Lord really cares for me, or do I think I need to control life and secure power so I don't need to trust? Do I really know what I need?" Like the Israelites in the desert, something in our souls does not want manna for today. We want the future wrapped in a bow *right now* so we can rest and not need to lay down our control and worry at God's feet.

This exposes how little we want to rely on God, and as we pray for our daily bread, we are conditioning our requests not only in reliance on his provision but also in the goodness of this reality. We find it easier to accept that we must rely on the Lord's sustenance than to accept it as good. We would rather rely on ourselves. Few lies are as foolish as this—that our lives are better off in our hands than in his—but if that is in our hearts, we must come to him here. So we pray, "Father, you know me so well. You know how much I would rather be at peace and at ease in myself rather than having to trust in you. Thank you for your gentle kindness in seeing all of this faithlessness and forgiving it all. Here I am. Have mercy on me and lead me into your faithfulness."

The second petition is for forgiveness. This request conditions our prayers by mirroring the forgiveness we so desperately want but so hesitantly give. We might hear this petition as follows: "God, let me forgive as you forgive." We know God forgives us completely, and we know our forgiving others falls short. This petition is a simple request that we might grow in being a forgiving person like God. But that is not the request. Rather, this challenges the whole of our petitionary life for others. Listen again: "God, forgive us our sins (or our debts) as we also forgive those who sin against us (or are our debtors)!"

This is different from what our hearts want to hear. Immediately our conscience pangs at these words. *Do I really want God to forgive me as I forgive others? No!* We don't want any comparison between God's forgiveness and our own. We forgive those who sin against us so poorly, slowly, and stingily. What we want is lavish forgiveness and lavish love, but we don't want to give it. We want it for ourselves. We want it to flow to us and stop, and we don't want to overflow in these ways. We must pray, "Father, have mercy, how do I forgive lavishly? How can I?"

As we pray for others, we may discover that all kinds of hidden feelings motivate our prayers for them. We pray for someone's conversion, growth, or situation in life, in part motivated by our unresolved feelings toward them. We may feel deep hurt, anger, resentment, or fatigue, and these may color our petitions on their behalf. We pray for them but do so hoping they won't be such a pain or hassle in our lives. As our prayers are formed by praying the Lord's Prayer truthfully, we should be awakened to what is going on in our relationships with those for whom we pray. We may discover a bitterness in our prayer that needs to be trans-formed by forgiveness. The petition for forgiveness should alter what and how we pray on their behalf. Our prayers may become softened, renewed, or more reflective of what is really good for them based on our new awareness and humility. We may become open to them in a new way, and we may be surprised to discover that what they really need is rather different from what we thought they—or *we*—needed.

We must hold our requests to God open in light of this petition to forgive as God has forgiven. We can now see our request in a new light. God's forgiveness is lavish, but it only flows forth from us as we attend to how much we really do need forgiveness and how little we want to forgive. The one who is forgiven little loves little (Luke 7:47), so we hold open our request and see how much we need to be forgiven in our envy, anger, and greed. Rather than being afraid of our faithlessness, recognizing our need for forgiveness helps us fulfill our calling to love. In light of how much we need forgiveness and how abundant the Lord's grace has been, we pray, "Father, forgive."

The third and final petition takes all we have requested and hears it in light of what Paul calls "the present evil age" (Gal. 1:4). This petition is also a reminder that, like Israel, we have been delivered from the land of slavery and are now in a wilderness of testing. We pray, "Our Father, please do not lead me into temptation, but deliver me from evil" (or "the evil one"). The word *temptation* is used either negatively, as we normally talk about being tempted, or positively, as in being tested. When we undergo this kind of testing, God refines and purifies our trust in him. But a testing becomes a negative temptation when the situation turns into something that tempts us away from God. This request is, therefore, an expression of need, an acknowledgment of weakness, and a hope that God will carefully watch over our situation. This is like a husband or wife saying, "Don't ever leave me." They are not verbalizing a worry that their spouse will leave; they are naming a longing to always remain together. This petition is a hope-filled recognition of our frailty before our caring Father. This is to pray a paraphrase of Psalm 103:14: "O Lord, know my frame; remember that I am dust."

At the core of this final petition we are asking, "God, I really don't know what is best to ask for, so please do not allow this to take me or others to a place that leads us away from you. Rather, deliver us from evil and the evil one in all the things for which I am asking. In all my prayers and in everything going on, lead me away from evil and guide me into your will for my life." The older I (John) am getting, the more precious this final petition has become. I now dwell on this a bit more and pray, "God, please, please do not lead me, my family, or those I know into places that will draw us away from you." Life is such a delicate balance of things that can happen and choices that are made that slowly take us in destructive directions. We don't know where our prayers and requests would take us if they were granted, so we pray, "God, keep us, preserve us, protect us from the evil one."

All our requests and petitions are, at their core, appeals for God's mercy and protection. The world and our own sinful desires are enemy enough, but we recognize that our lives are lived on a spiritual battleground. As Paul reminds us, "For we do not wrestle against flesh and blood, but against the rulers, against the authorities, against the cosmic powers over this present darkness, against the spiritual forces of evil in the heavenly places" (Eph. 6:12). As he goes on to admonish us to put on the armor of God, he tells us to pray "at all times in the Spirit, with all prayer and supplication" (v. 18). In our petition to be delivered and led by the Lord, we recall the spiritual reality of our prayers to once again allow our own desires to be revealed.

To pray the Lord's Prayer is to enter into a prayer of another—of our Lord—that leads us into a world to which we belong, but one that is still foreign. We struggle against the fact that our eyes are still oriented to the dark, when the Lord has called us into the light. We pray in truth, but we do so as those watchful of our hearts, holding our petitions to God in light of this prayer. As we do so, we should seek to have Jesus's prayer in Gethsemane condition all of our prayers: "Not my will, but yours, be done" (Luke 22:42).

As we internalize the Lord's Prayer, we recognize that it does not contain all we will ask of God; it does not set limits on our praying. Rather, it has the possibility of conditioning and shaping all we have to ask and say to inform and lead us into a more profound experience of talking to our Father in heaven. As we pray the closing of the Lord's Prayer, as many of us learned it ("For thine is the kingdom, and the power, and the glory forever. Amen"), we use this to name the truth of what it means to pray "not my will, but yours, be done." For the kingdom is not mine, but his. The power is not mine, but his. The glory is not mine, but his. That is the reality that challenges and confronts our fantasies about our own kingdom, power, and glory that so often color our prayers.

PRACTICE

The Lord's Prayer

As we conclude this interlude, take a petition or request you have been praying for that really matters to you and let each phrase of the Lord's Prayer condition your prayer. So, for example, if you have been asking the Lord for a job you desperately need or for him to heal a hurting relationship, take five or ten minutes to go through each phrase and let the truth of the Lord's Prayer condition and instruct you on how to keep praying for that particular issue. Be open to the truth of your motivations and deep desires and to your Father and his desires in all of this.

Our Father in heaven,
hallowed be your name.
Your kingdom come,
your will be done,
on earth as it is in heaven.
Give us this day our daily bread,
and forgive us our debts,
as we also have forgiven our debtors.
And lead us not into temptation,
but deliver us from evil.
For yours is the kingdom,
the power, and the glory,
forever and ever.
Amen.

PART 2

Pray without Ceasing

INTRODUCTION

A New Rhythm of Prayer

I n this second section, we shift gears a bit and take a more practical turn to prayer. Each chapter provides an overview of a type of prayer, and following each chapter is a short practice section to help you pray. Our hope is that these prayers refresh not only your time in prayer but also the entirety of your life with God. These forms of prayer are ways to embrace the journey of faith, hope, and love the Lord calls us to. But you must ask yourself, "Am I open to this deeper journey with the Lord? Do I really want a deeper life of prayer, or do I simply want something to 'fix' my praying and make it 'work'?" If so, even this is an invitation to a deeper way.

The five forms of prayer we are introducing are praying the Psalms, prayers of intention, prayers of recollection, prayers of examine, and prayers of intercession. This may seem a bit overwhelming. Do not start by adding all these into your life. Take some time to discern how you should proceed in light of where the Lord has you in life, what you believe he has called you to, and the history of your prayer life. Consider how these prayers are meant to form certain virtues and characteristics of your praying.

We believe all these prayers should be part of a Christian's prayer life, but there's not a need to pray them all daily. As a starting point, pray a psalm daily as you continue to read this book. As you work through the following chapters, consider one other form of prayer to integrate into your life now. Start there. Attend to how you experience these forms of prayer and how you naturally judge these experiences as "good" or "bad." This is a retraining in not only *how* to pray but also your expectations about the Christian life entirely.

It is also important to consider that these forms of prayer can easily devolve into the old, fallen machinery of the heart we discussed in part 1. In the flesh, these prayers can become new places to hide, cover, and placate our guilt. They can become places where we avoid honesty, try to manage an angry God, or attempt to feel better about our spiritual lives. All we discussed earlier must be brought to these forms of prayer as well. No form is impervious to our sinful and broken strategies. Every act can be commandeered by our fleshly ways. We must keep our eyes and hearts attuned to the Lord as we practice them so they will help us be honest with God as he transforms our hearts.

Let this be an invitation to draw near to the Lord deeply, honestly, and intentionally. Consider how your prayer has or has not been based on reality in your life or how much of your prayer life has been formed by attempts at placating or even domesticating God. Allow the truth of your heart to be opened, regardless of what you find there. Trust that the Lord is big enough, loving enough, and forgiving enough to hear, see, and forgive. As a Father calls a child to himself seeking the truth of the child's heart, so the Lord has called you to himself. He is your Father seeking you as his child. Pray from this place.

5

The Prayer Book of the Soul

I (John) recall a three-month period when my wife and I prayed a psalm in the morning and a psalm in the evening, six days a week. We simply started with the psalm, did not look where it was going, and prayed. Due to difficult circumstances in my life, the varying experiences of the psalmists, and how the Spirit was teaching us with these words, this became an experiential roller-coaster ride with my soul and my wife. It was a precious time for us together and was profoundly meaningful during a difficult season. The Psalms are a gift to the people of God to shepherd us in the confusing realities of this world.

Christians have always recognized the profound role the Psalms play in the Christian life. John Calvin called the Psalms "an anatomy of all the parts of the soul," while early church Father Athanasius claimed that "the Book of Psalms possesses somehow the perfect image for the soul's course of life."[1] In Calvin's estimation, the Psalms reveal to us the full range of our emotional lives, just as Athanasius believed the Psalms teach us the remedy for our broken hearts. The Psalms are a mirror that helps us see what life with God is like; therefore, they serve to guide and shepherd our praying so we can be with our Father in the full truth of our lives.

As we pray through the Psalms, we may experience an odd tension between the brutal honesty of the psalmist (Ps. 137:9) and Jesus's call to love our enemies and pray for those who persecute us (Matt. 5:44). The Psalms call us into parts of ourselves we don't want to see, and certainly don't want the Lord to see, that actually seem contradictory to his calling on our lives. This is just a small glimpse into the tensions we face. Only in praying the Psalms do we experience the full range of tensions they call us into, inviting us to wrestle through the truth of ourselves in honesty before God.

The Psalms are not to be prayed as a magical formula or as calm, calculated theology about a God who, though real, is distant and safe. Rather, they call us before the true God we find in Scripture, a God who is entirely free and holy. As the hymnal for the people of God, the Psalms do provide a deep theology of God but not always in the usual sense. They teach us about who God is by telling us what he can hear.

We discover a lot about a person based on what they can hear. It turns out that God can hear wonderful things, delightful things, hard things, angry things, and frustrating things. God can even hear false accusations and false claims. The Psalms are filled with all of these. When God's people speak out of their pain, they often speak things that are not necessarily true about reality but are true of how they experience reality. The Psalms reveal that God wants to hear what his people feel, even when, maybe especially when, what we feel seems too difficult to share. This tells us much about who our God is.

Abiding and Humility in Prayer

In 2 Corinthians 12, Paul gives us a glimpse of his own wrestling with God in prayer. After walking the Corinthians through his struggles in ministry, he tells them about a "thorn" in his flesh, specifically a messenger of Satan who harasses him (see 2 Cor. 11:16–33; 12:1–7). After all of Paul's struggles, and after all he had given for the proclamation of the gospel, Paul was stuck dealing with this messenger of Satan. So what did Paul do? He prayed. He pleaded with the Lord to take this away from him three times, but the Lord refused (2 Cor. 12:8).

God did not take this thorn away from Paul for two reasons. First, it was meant to keep him from becoming conceited (2 Cor. 12:7). Second, as the risen and ascended Lord told him, in response to his pleading, "My grace is sufficient for you, for my power is made perfect in weakness" (2 Cor. 12:9). What Paul asked to have taken away from him was actually a gift from God. God "gifted" Paul with struggles so he would abide and embrace humility. Paul needed this thorn, whatever it was, to help orient him to God and God's power and away from himself and his own power. The Lord's goal for Paul wasn't to rid him of anything that bothered him. The Lord led Paul to himself in the truth of his struggling because the goal was Paul's abiding and humility.

We should expect this same reality in our own praying. In reflecting on what this means for us, Puritan theologian John Owen writes about a believer begging God to remove his lust. Owen then writes, "God says, 'Here is one, if he could be rid of this lust I should never hear of him more; let him wrestle with this, or he is lost.'"[2] What John Owen is pointing to, and what Paul had to realize, is that if God took away our struggles and, at times, even our sin, then we would no longer come to him. God calls us to abide in him so we can bear much fruit and know him as our strength. Yet we are tempted to seek God to take away our sins so we don't have to abide. Maybe having a "good" and "exciting" experience in prayer at this time in your life would be the worst thing for your abiding. Maybe mastering a prayer method would undermine God's work. Maybe the experience of failure in prayer is exactly how we come to understand that God's power is made perfect in our weakness. Many of us haven't wrestled with or even considered the truth that if God did grant our prayers to "take this sin away from me," maybe we would cease praying and depending on him.

Consider your life. When are you most prayerful? Is it in satisfaction or in struggle? Why? In good times, do you pray less and with less intensity because you do not feel your need? In our satisfaction, we have the illusion of being able to navigate life on our own. We can even think we can minister, love our neighbor, and serve without abiding and without prayer. Lord, have mercy! Our trials and difficulties, however, often bring us back to our inability and our need for the Lord to intervene. In these spaces, we know the truth that the Lord is calling us to be with him, to abide in him, and to know that without him we can do nothing (John 15:5). Paul had to learn how to wrestle with God in prayer, and the thorn helped make this possible. This wrestling is the kind of praying the Psalms lead us into.

As we seek to be faithful, we, too, find ourselves wrestling with God. *Why didn't you heal this person? Why didn't you make my pain go away? Why is this person in my life? Why don't you change this? Why!?* While we often want the wrestling to just go away, the Lord has a gift in it for us, even if it is a gift we don't want. The wrestling itself is important. Naming ways our hearts are not like the Lord's is necessary for praying through his Word. This is why the Psalms only frustrate the person looking for a tidy description of God or the Christian life.

Praying the Psalms unveils the ways we want prayer to be simpler, and maybe even simplistic, and they push us into tension. On the one hand, the psalmist praises God for his steadfast covenant love (Pss. 105, 106), while on the other, he asserts that God has forgotten his covenant loyalty (Pss. 13, 77, 88). *Well, which is it?* When we were seminary students, we found this infuriating or, if nothing else, spiritually confusing. At the same time, we were growing frustrated with the Bible's prayer book and becoming prayerless.

In our prayerlessness and our failure to pray through the Psalms, we were unable to appreciate the truths of God implicit in what God can hear. These apparent tensions in the Psalms begin to make sense only in the *experience* of honest prayer. In coming out of hiding, you will come to realize that you often have conflicting feelings and thoughts about God, yourself, and prayer. Sharing these feelings is part of abiding. Sharing these struggles affirms that God can hear them, and that he already knows them, even before you pray. We both discovered how profound the Psalms were later in life, when prayer led us into our frustration and anger. We realized with the psalmists that God wanted to hear all that was in our hearts. This led us to pray, "Father, I don't think you want to hear what is on my heart, particularly the things that do not please you." We discovered the Psalms were a training ground for lifting our hearts up to the Lord.

Invitation: Praying the Psalms

Psalms are the inspired prayers of God's people that inform us how to talk to God in all the seasons of our spiritual lives. While there are many ways to understand the nature and movement of the Psalter, we have found Walter Brueggemann's characterization helpful. According to Brueggemann, generally speaking, there are three kinds of psalms for three kinds of seasons in our spiritual lives: psalms of orientation, disorientation, and reorientation.[3] Following God leads us into experiences of orientation, disorientation, and reorientation in our lives, and each of these realities is apparent in almost every psalm.[4] While we talk about these categories as defining whole psalms in this section, it is important to remember that these experiences are woven throughout most of the Psalms individually.

Jesus uniquely discovered his life and mission detailed in the pages of the Psalter. As Jesus took these Psalms to be his own, he located himself in God's presence and redemption. Jesus experienced the disorientation of the cross, utilizing Psalm 22 to find words to name his sorrow with the Father. Jesus used the Psalms to reorient his disciples after his resurrection, showing them how the Psalms must be fulfilled (Luke 24:44). It was through the Psalms that Jesus prayed about his calling as the Son of God and about what it meant to be the suffering servant of God. Only Jesus could really pray some of the Psalms as they were meant to be prayed. In them he learned to share the most raw and honest feelings of hurt, frustration, misunderstanding, rejection, and anger—while growing in how to love, care for, and forgive the very enemies he struggled with (cf. Ps. 69). For those of us willing to pray the Psalms honestly from the heart, this will be the journey for us as well.

The Psalms provide a way to pray through all the various facets of our hearts, precisely because the life of Jesus, a life that we are now part of, is the life the Spirit is forming us into. Jesus had the joy of loving parents and the confusion of not seeing eye to eye with them (Luke 2:49). Jesus knew what it meant to have friends and what it was like to be mocked and despised (Ps. 69:7–12, 20–21). Jesus knew temptation, rejection, and the experience of abandonment, and he knew the union of love with his Father and the presence of the Spirit. Jesus, in Gethsemane, knew what it was like to struggle with God in prayer. Jesus experienced wrestling with what it meant to be faithful in the face of evil, fully aware that his will differed from his Father's.

As they did for Jesus, the Psalms help us locate ourselves in God's redemption. The Psalms, like the Lord's Prayer, help to condition and shape our praying. Even though these are set prayers—they are in their final form—our prayers are not. Just as in Jesus's use of them, the words of the Psalms must become our own. These prayers form our hearts to pray to our Father in the Son and by the Spirit. In every season of the Christian journey, whether mountaintop or desert wandering, the Psalms provide prayers to shepherd our hearts to our Father.

As we think about this invitation to pray through the Psalms regularly, we need to consider what it means to pray through our orientation, disorientation, and reorientation to God. While every Psalm should instill faith, hope, and love in our hearts, each of these three orientations emphasizes one of these specifically. Psalms of orientation are psalms of faith, because they name the truth of God's world when his ways are not clear to our sight. We walk by faith in the kingdom, and not by sight, because Jesus calls us to the unseen reality of God's way. We affirm in faith that God's way is truly *the way* and seek to live and pray according to that reality.

Psalms of disorientation are psalms of hope because they call us to name our struggles, pains, and longings to God in hopes that he hears and with the hope of his redemption. As he did with Paul in 2 Corinthians 12, God might not take us out of this disorientation immediately, but these psalms point us to our true hope. It was for "the joy that was set before" Jesus—his *hoping* for joy—that he endured the disorientation of the cross (Heb. 12:2).

The psalms of reorientation are psalms of love, because they give us a glimpse of the movement of our lives through trials to the day when God will be all in all and where "we shall be like him, because we shall see him as he is" (1 John 3:2). Psalms of reorientation help us bask in the truth that our God of love will make all things right and that love will endure forever because the greatest of these—faith, hope, and love—is love (1 Cor. 13:13).

Orientation in Faith

Psalms of orientation affirm the ways God has made the world work. Some of these will be apparent to us; therefore, we can rest in faith that the Lord governs his world according to his laws. We look out and see that the unjust are punished and the godly are rewarded; we know by faith that God is on the throne, regardless of what the world claims; and we can rest in the Lord's work in our lives and see his good fruit. All is well-ordered. Life in the presence of God is good.

These psalms of orientation include praise psalms (such as Ps. 33 and Ps. 150) but also wisdom psalms (such as Ps. 1). These psalms encourage us to pray and stay open to God, to praise him, and to trust that God has ordered life well for his people. The corrective we discover in this, when all is going well, is that we might be tempted to stop praying to and relying on God. In difficult times, we may not feel like praying these psalms or praising God, but they are nonetheless still true, and it is good for us to know this. In faith, they raise our souls to something greater than our trials and open us to a deeper abiding in God. At times, however, our souls will be vexed by these prayers because they seem so contrary to our feelings.

One difficulty in praying these psalms is how easy it is to pray the truth simply because it is in the Bible without ever considering if we really believe it is true. We may be praying Psalm 84,

> How lovely is your dwelling place,
>   O Lord of hosts!
> My soul longs, yes, faints
>   for the courts of the Lord;   .
> my heart and flesh sing for joy
>   to the living God. . . .
>
> For a day in your courts is better
>   than a thousand elsewhere. (vv. 1–2, 10)

Do we really believe a day in God's courts is better than a thousand elsewhere? How might we pray this while attending to the truth of our hearts as a prayer of faith? What would it mean to live in this world as if this were true? For some, praying this psalm makes their heart come alive. For these folks, the temptation is to think this will always be true. If they go to pray this beloved psalm again and their heart does not respond, they are now tempted to generate an experience with passion rather than open their heart to the Lord.

Some of us pray this psalm and it doesn't awaken anything in us. We're not even sure what it means. We wonder if one day in God's courts are better than a thousand elsewhere. If this is true of you, you need to pay attention to the temptation to either pass over this prayer or deceive yourself into assuming it is true of you. You may be tempted to make this psalm a prayer of magic, where you assume that as long as you say the right formula, usually with the right zeal, it will become true. Or, alternatively, we can think that if we pray hard enough, God will heal our souls like he heals limbs and we won't have to experience the truth of our pain, sin, and brokenness. Too many of us simply exclaim Scripture is true without ever realizing that our hearts are elsewhere.

Instead of keeping this in the abstract, take a moment to pray these words from Psalm 33 and see what it does in your soul. What is it like for you right now to simply praise God for who he is and what he has done?

> Sing joyfully to the LORD, you righteous;
>   it is fitting for the upright to praise him.
> Praise the LORD with the harp;
>   make music to him on the ten-stringed lyre.
> Sing to him a new song;
>   play skillfully, and shout for joy.
>
> For the word of the LORD is right and true;
>   he is faithful in all he does.
> The LORD loves righteousness and justice;
>   the earth is full of his unfailing love. (vv. 1–5 NIV)

You may find these words reflective of what is going on in your soul right now and be able to breathe them out easily as an overflow of your heart. If this is so, praise God.

Alternatively, you may find this prayer of praise entirely incongruent to what is going on in your heart. You may find it difficult to praise God due to trials you are experiencing or some kind of spiritual distress. These words may feel dry as dust for your thirsty or tired soul. That is good to know as well! This is an opportunity to let these words be a mirror to your heart. Let the psalm open your heart to a real conversation with God. Tell him the truth about what is going on in your soul and let him love you and teach you in these realities. Allow these psalms to orient your heart to the goodness of God and his provision for you. No matter how your heart responds, use that as the content of your prayer—whether it is joy, lament, thankfulness, anger, guilt, or shame.

Disorientation for Hope

Life, of course, is more complicated than discovering the truth and orienting ourselves to it, as if we were robots that simply needed the right coding. The Psalms reveal that life looks very different from this. In fact, the greatest percentage of the Psalms are psalms of disorientation. These are prayers for seasons of anguish, hurt, frustration, anger, alienation, suffering, and confusion. These prayers assist with present torment and anguish, but they may also spur us to come out of hiding and experience what is really going on in our hearts. We hear the call in these psalms only as we begin to make the words our own, entering into the prayer of another and learning to voice the truth of our hearts. These psalms teach us to voice our own disorientation in God's world and help us enter into the disorientation of others.

The most abundant of all the Psalms are *lament* psalms, which are complaints to God. These contain regret, self-loathing, anger, and even hatred toward others. Sometimes these psalms include accusations and anger toward God. I (John) find these psalms of disorientation interesting and alluring, because they point out so acutely what little guidance I had regarding how to pray in such an honest way. I was taught to study and obey, but I had little understanding of how I could pray during difficult times. The first twenty-five years of my spiritual life, I tried to pray everything as a psalm of orientation, almost trying to will it to be true. This betrayed the truth, of course. Not all my experiences were of orientation.

Upon reflection, it appears I used prayer as an attempt to re-translate my experience into times of orientation—where God was good and would make things fine—as a way to tell myself everything would be okay. But this wasn't always true. I wasn't able to look squarely at the state of my soul and pray what was there, because I didn't think God wanted to hear that. My prayers became attempts to control God and my circumstances apart from the way things actually are. For a young believer, these prayers may be appropriate—I probably wasn't ready to talk with God about all the messy stuff in my soul—but in my growth I had to learn how to leave childish ways behind so I could press into maturity.

These prayers only make sense if, when we pray them, we are open to experience the truth of our hearts with God. Pause for a moment and see what happens in your soul as you make this prayer your own:

> My guilt has overwhelmed me
> > like a burden too heavy to bear.
>
> My wounds fester and are loathsome
> > because of my sinful folly.
> I am bowed down and brought very low;
> > all day long I go about mourning.
> My back is filled with searing pain;
> > there is no health in my body.
> I am feeble and utterly crushed;
> > I groan in anguish of heart.

All my longings lie open before you, Lord
   my sighing is not hidden from you.
My heart pounds, my strength fails me;
   even the light has gone from my eyes. (Ps. 38:4–10 NIV)

In the early days of my faith, my guilt would not have allowed me to pray such a prayer. Like guilt did for Adam and Eve, my guilt led me away from God, and I saw God as a problem that needed to be managed. It would have been so good to bring my self-loathing, regret, groanings, and sufferings to God—not cleaned up and made neat but in their unvarnished truth. Instead, I tried to pray "rightly."

Even if I could have prayed these psalms of lament, however, I think I would have tried to resolve them too quickly. Instead of wrestling with God in the truth of my soul, I worry that I would have moved into a godless hope. This is not a hope in God but a naive wish that everything will be okay as long as I think positively. This is similar to what Paul calls "worldly grief," in comparison with "godly grief" over our sin: "For godly grief produces a repentance that leads to salvation without regret, whereas worldly grief produces death" (2 Cor. 7:10). Too often we see our brokenness and the brokenness of our lives and turn to worldly grief. This is why it is important not to move too quickly to resolution or repentance. We are tempted to grieve our brokenness and sin in the flesh, which is simply a strategy for moving on and hoping for the best. We have to enter into the truth of ourselves and trust that God has not only forgiven me in these places but is also interceding for me there. It is easy to repent of something we haven't fully seen in ourselves. Repentance can quickly become another tool of managing and worldly grieving.

While this prayer may not reflect where you are now, file it away for a time when it can speak what is in your heart. If it does capture a season you have journeyed through, but you did not pray honestly about it when you were in this season, this could be a time to open up the old questions, feelings, and thoughts that may still reside in your heart. How can you enter into those things with the Lord and grieve them in him and with him?

However, this prayer may perfectly capture the current state of your spiritual confusion, your self-hatred for what you have done or become, or your spiritual "faintings" for how weak you feel in light of your failings. I know this well now, and these psalms have become both painful and solace to my soul as I pray these matters to God. All of us, at some point, have to wrestle through the fact that the Christian life is not what we expected. God is not the God we imagined he would be. God does things we don't know what to do with. No honest reading of Scripture leaves us with a God who meets all our expectations. Rather, God confounds us. As he does so, he offers us a book of prayers that teach us how to lament and complain to God about God himself! His ways are not our ways indeed.

These prayers teach us to pray about how distant God has felt, how it feels like he no longer cares, or how it seems as though he doesn't hear our prayers at all. Rather than closing down our prayer life in the midst of these responses, it is so much better to honestly pray with the psalmist,

> How long, Lord? Will you forget me forever?
> How long will you hide your face from me?
> How long must I wrestle with my thoughts
> and day after day have sorrow in my heart?
> How long will my enemy triumph over me? (Ps. 13:1–2 NIV)

> I remembered you, God, and I groaned;
> I meditated, and my spirit grew faint.
> You kept my eyes from closing;
> I was too troubled to speak.
> I thought about the former days,
> the years of long ago;

I remembered my songs in the night.
My heart meditated and my spirit asked:

"Will the Lord reject forever?
    Will he never show his favor again?
Has his unfailing love vanished forever?
    Has his promise failed for all time?
Has God forgotten to be merciful?
    Has he in anger withheld his compassion?"
        (Ps. 77:3–9 NIV)

But I cry to you for help, LORD;
    in the morning my prayer comes before you.
Why, LORD, do you reject me
    and hide your face from me? (Ps. 88:13–14 NIV)

As we pray these, the first thing that should strike us is not only how honest these complaints are but also that the people of God are given divine permission to pray false statements to God. God has not forgotten his covenant or his people. He calls us to pray through the truth of how we feel and think, so we must, like the psalmist, take what is in our souls and put that into words in prayer. These statements are still true, of course—they are the true cries of his people. Remember what we said earlier: what God sees is what he can hear, and this is what we should talk with him about.

If I had prayed the Psalms rather than studied them, I would have understood the simple truth that these are the prayers of God's people during times of spiritual dryness and confusion. These psalms were the training ground I needed to navigate these seasons, where I could turn to the Psalms in my own feelings of abandonment, just as Jesus prayed Psalm 22:1: "My God, my God, why have you forsaken me?" (Matt. 27:46). Through this I come to understand that these psalms of disorientation tell us, in the words of Brueggemann,

There is nothing out of bounds in prayer, nothing precluded or inappropriate. Everything properly belongs in the conversation of the heart with God. To withhold parts of life from that conversation is in fact to withhold part of it from the sovereignty of God. Thus, the Psalms make the important connection: everything must be *brought to speech*, and everything brought to speech must be *addressed to God*, who is the final reference for all of life.[5]

Praying these psalms in the disorientation of our lives leads us to embrace hope, knowing that the Christian life will always have wanderings in the desert. We hope because we follow a God who did not avoid our darkness but descended into it. In the words of Todd Billings in his wonderful book on lament, "For while the psalms of lament are psalms of confusion, anger, and fear, they are also psalms of hope—prayers that come before God in hope, making a plea for him to show himself faithful to his promises."[6]

Reorientation in Love

While we are tempted in seasons of disorientation to move on as quickly as possible, that isn't our call as Christians. The question should not be, "How do I get out of here?" but rather "Lord, what does it mean to be faithful here?" or "Lord, how can I abide in you and your love in this place, which feels so disorienting?" As we abide in disorientation, we trust that the Lord is not leading us into wandering for its own sake but is shepherding us into his rest (even if we must go through the desert to get there). Psalms of reorientation form us for this rest, building on the faith and hope cultivated through seasons of orientation and disorientation. Just like in a close friendship, things change after strife and reconciliation. We, too, are changed when we are granted the reorienting mercies of God.

Psalms of reorientation are prayers for times when things are bad and not going well, but then God in his goodness and joy breaks through the despair and surprises us with a season of renewal and peace. These are prayers of thanksgiving for answered prayers and prayers of love as we come to further embrace the realities of life with God. Take, for instance, Psalm 40, and once again, make these words your own to God as you draw near to him:

> I waited patiently for the LORD;
>   he inclined to me and heard my cry.
> He drew me up from the pit of destruction,
>   out of the miry bog;
> and set my feet upon a rock,
>   making my steps secure.
> He put a new song in my mouth,
>   a song of praise to our God.
> Many will see and fear,
>   and put their trust in the LORD. (vv. 1–3)

These words were written to encourage us to pray when we are in a new season of joy after a trial has passed. Many of us are tempted to pray zealously in a trial, only to stop praying when things get better. These prayers remind us of times past when God did profoundly restorative work in our lives, and now they reawaken that memory with thanksgiving. If we pray these prayers in seasons of sorrow, as some of us may, they can touch our hearts with hope, but they may also mirror unrequited desire and bring increased awareness of pain when hope is low. Whatever we are going through as we pray them, these prayers serve to mirror something of our soul back to us, so we can bring these things to God. In this way, these prayers reorient us to the journey of love we are called to by the Lord, where by faith and hope we have set our eyes on the city where every tear will be wiped away (Rev. 21:4) and where God will quiet us by his love (Zeph. 3:17). What is your heart's response to the words of Scripture? This is what we can take to God. We may not currently experience the love of God, or we may be currently overwhelmed by it. These prayers help ground us in the truth that the Christian life is a journey of love that never ceases.

Some of us will struggle to make the words of the Psalms our own. This is true of every worship song we have ever sung, as we use the words of another to praise God. Taking on the words of the Psalms can keep us in prayer when we struggle to pray and undermines the temptation to stop praying. The Psalms force us into rich and often weighty questions in our souls, and they offer a structure to prayer that can help us enter it deeply. Be particularly attentive to which psalms are difficult to pray and ways to make every psalm a prayer of orientation (or, for that matter, disorientation or reorientation). God has greater things for you than lip service. He invites you to embrace the Psalms as the school of prayer for your soul.

PRACTICE

Praying the Psalms

For your own practice, take ten minutes or so and do one of the suggestions below. Or take twenty to thirty minutes and practice each of these. We especially encourage you to make this a habit for 150 days or approximately five months. Take a psalm a day and pray it in the morning. This kind of practice has proven profoundly helpful for us both.

There are, broadly, two ways to enter into this practice of praying the Psalms. The first is to simply start praying the Psalter one psalm at a time. For many, praying a psalm a day is the beginning of a devoted time in Scripture or in prayer. Read through the psalm once to get a sense of its movements, and then pray back through it slowly, seeking to make the words your own. This initial reading can help orient your heart to the themes you will be confronted with as you enter into prayer.

Alternatively, instead of reading through the psalm first, you may want to just pray into the psalm without knowing where it is leading. This approach may help you enter more fully and experientially into the prayer, letting the psalmist take you on an unexpected journey through your soul by means of his words. In both cases, it can be helpful to pray aloud, always attending to how your heart is responding. *Is this something true of my soul? Does my heart want to reject praying this to the Lord?* The words of Psalm 139:23–24 are helpful to come back to here: "Search me, O God, and know my heart! Try me and know my thoughts! And see if there be any grievous way in me, and lead me in the way everlasting!"

Along the way, as you pray through the words of the psalmist, you may need to pause to translate the words into your own experience. Often, in praying the Psalms, I (John) pray something that strikes my heart and speaks into a specific circumstance I am wrestling with. When this happens, I pause and, in my own words, pray through the circumstance in the manner of the psalm. I no longer pray generically about my struggles but enter into the reality of *this particular* struggle as the words of the psalmist open my heart to this kind of prayer to God.

The second approach to praying the Psalms is to go directly to a psalm that fits your particular life circumstances. This can be a helpful practice to speak the truth of your experience and learn ways to express the truth of your soul to God, even when aspects of the psalm may not be true of your circumstance. For this purpose, we have a listing of several of these in appendix 1 and directions for making these words your own. Our hope is to help model how you can form your own experiences into prayers.

6

Intending to Be with God

Several years ago, it became clear that every time I (John) would wake up, morning after morning, my heart would automatically take me in one direction or another. My heart was like a compass needle, immediately seeking north to my true desires, worries, and fears. My mind would immediately go to things that weighed on me, and these thoughts revealed something true of me. I am a worrier. Instead of getting up and putting on clothes, my heart would wake and put on worry. I often worried before I went to bed and, like a close traveling companion, worry would revisit me upon waking. Worry is when our fears move us to ourselves and our own resources to fix our problems. We believe that if we take our eyes off the problem, no one, including God, will attend to it. The essence of worry is distrust in God; distrust is the intention of the heart trained in worry.

I didn't worry on purpose. This wasn't something I consciously did, as if I sat in bed for a moment, still groggy from the night before, and thought to myself, *You know, I should worry about something.* Most mornings it was so automatic that I didn't notice.

Worry was the first movement of my heart, revealing deep and abiding intentions in my character. But it wasn't only worry. Whatever was bothering me in the day, whatever tasks I had to do, as soon as I would wake up, my mind would immediately go to them. When Jesus said, "Where your treasure is, there your heart will be also" (Matt. 6:21), he was giving us a way to understand where our hearts naturally turn us. Why was the true north of my soul worry, and what could I do about it?

There came a moment several years ago when I thought to myself, *I'm tired of doing this. I want to open to the Lord the first thing in the morning.* I was tired of the sin habits of my soul setting the agenda for my day and immediately going to my troubles. I was fed up with my heart's broken intentions. That is when I told the Lord I wanted to "intend" my day differently. Behind this was Dallas Willard's notion that whenever the Scriptures give you a command or a task to do, you can translate it into a "spiritual discipline" or training.[1] In light of my situation, I took the command in Romans to present myself to God (Rom. 6:13) and translated it into a prayer of intention. The prayer of intention is a way to intentionally direct or, better, redirect my heart at the very dawn of my day. I wanted to relearn how to walk with the Spirit rather than walking in the old habits of the flesh. This prayer guides us into that retraining.

Unfortunately, we tend to let the already trained habits and intentions of our hearts dictate what we think. The problem is, each moment triggers and awakens prior trainings of our hearts that we have imbibed. My own heart has been trained in worry; it has also been trained in anger. So, it is unsurprising that I quickly turn to these things. Whether we are confronted with a joyful reality (e.g., a wedding, a birth, a new job) or a sorrow-filled reality (e.g., unemployment, the death of a loved one, a scary diagnosis), our hearts immediately turn to their training. This programming of our hearts leads us to our own internal resources as coping strategies and not to Christ. What the heart needs is a *retraining* in faith, hope, and love of the Lord. We must begin with a conscious intention to redirect our hearts to the Lord.

Retraining in Christ

Even though we have committed our lives to Christ, we may not have experienced a retraining of our hearts in the Lord. Most of us simply follow the training of our youth, likely a training with little intention, and continue to employ it. Some of our training has served us well in life, at least practically speaking, while other parts of it have deeply failed us. In both success and failure, we turn to this training without thinking. This training forms subconscious scripts that determine how we respond to life. These need to be transformed in the Lord.

As kids, Kyle and I were both trained in sports to use anger, determination, and fortitude to dominate and win. Unsurprisingly, when we got to Bible college, seminary, and then ministry, that is exactly the training we utilized for success. We dominated and won Bible classes, tests, grades, and then ministry. But this doesn't work. It *really* does not work in prayer. So we rarely prayed. The training of our hearts betrayed us. We needed a retraining in the way of the Lord. The main practice field for this retraining, we would discover, is prayer.

The question we must ask is this: "How do I put off the deep, old, sinful trainings of my heart to put on the Lord (the 'new man') in all things [Eph. 4:22–24]?" We begin this putting off and putting on at the outset of the day, because right away our poorly trained hearts try to set the agenda. But this is just the beginning of an overall training that needs to continue throughout our day.

In this retraining, I have to be open to my anger when I am cut off by another driver on the freeway or when my kids disobey me or when life does not go the way I want, and I need to turn to the Lord first in light of the truth. I must ask, Lord, *why am I so angry? Why does my heart think I can will my life to work the way I want it to? Lord, I want life on my own terms. Lord, have mercy.*

Every day holds unanticipated surprises, so we must intend to be with the Lord in all things. We lead with our intention to be with God in the fullness of life so we can be present to what confronts us as an opportunity to turn to him. This might be the person at work who shames us, our child's friend whose influence scares us, or the upcoming doctor visit that worries us. We bring many things before the Lord to seek his guidance as to how we should be present to them.

I (Kyle) have chronic pain. So that it won't dominate my life, I naturally avoid thinking and worrying about it. But this makes my suffering meaningless. My pain becomes one more thing I navigate in the old training of my heart. In Christ, this pain can be a gift. Like the thorn in Paul's flesh, pain is not a gift I want, nor is it "good" in itself; it is still a kind of evil (a "messenger of Satan"). But in the Lord, it can serve a greater good, which is my utter dependence on God. This, too, can be part of my suffering with Christ that Paul speaks of (Rom. 8:17). Suffering in itself does not make me achieve dependence on Christ, as if suffering naturally oriented me to God. Rather, each day I have to ready myself to embrace this suffering in Christ, and not on my own. I need an intention to guide me to Jesus, or the deep, old training of my life will take over. When this happens, I simply try to muscle through the pain in hopes that it won't alter my life too much.

Present Yourself to God

Prayers of intention are guided by Paul's instructions in Romans 6:13: "Present yourselves to God as those who have been brought from death to life, and your members to God as instruments for righteousness." Similarly, Paul states, "I appeal to you therefore, brothers and sisters, by the mercies of God, to present your bodies as a living sacrifice, holy and acceptable to God, which is your spiritual worship" (Rom. 12:1 NRSV). Notice the focus on presenting ourselves to God. And more specifically, in that presenting, we are making an intention to live life with him. This is a prayer of presenting ourselves to God. As Christians, we have a deep intention and love of God in our souls. But this intention is often commandeered by the contrary habits and intentions of our hearts, formed in the flesh, to navigate life on our own.

Deep in my own heart, I (John) intend to rest on God, trust him, and seek him in all things. Yet first thing in the morning, my heart is doing something else. My heart is still trying to bear the weight of my life on its own, doing what it has always done. My habits need to be reconnected with the deeper intention of my heart so I can hand my entire life to God. I want to "incline my heart" to God's ways (Ps. 119:112) and to the deeper intention of my heart—to abide in him and not in my own resources.

Now I shut down what my heart grabs on to when I wake, and instead, I *intentionally* pray a prayer of intention: "Lord, here I am. I present myself to you. Before I do anything else, I first want to be with you." My initial move is not to find a solution to my worries. Rather, the first thing I need to do is intend to be with God. That means I intend to actually show up in his presence and not try to use God to have life on my terms. I want to be with God regardless of what he has planned for me. Nothing is simpler and more possible than this prayer of intention, and it has been such a gift and relief to me. When my worries, unsurprisingly, emerge, I once again refuse to continue down that road and instead come back to the prayer of intention: "Lord, here I am. I present myself to you!"

Admittedly, I may not be able to sustain my intention long. Because my character has been trained in fleshly ways over decades, when I am confronted with the troubles of the day, my heart automatically moves to the old habits of worry and fleshly control. I can't just make this go away. What I can do, all throughout my day, is present myself to the Lord with another new intention: "Stop, John, this is not the way. Lord, I again present myself to you. Here I am. Let's talk about this." Again and again, the Christian can find joy in being with the Lord in the midst of brokenness and rebellion, knowing his shepherding heart in those places of the flesh.

In being present to God, I am not ignoring what my heart wants from me, but rather I am recalling my heart to a deeper and more profound reality than my own desires and strategies for navigating life. But I can only bring those desires before God if I am honest about them. When I am confronted with my worry, I know part of that worry is the desire for control. I long for the ability to will the life I want into existence. I want to have life on my terms. I want to control how things turn out. So, as I present myself to God, to be with him, I present the truth of what is going on in my heart:

> *Father, look at these desires. In my flesh I want to have life on my own terms, in my own way, for my own ends. I am tempted to use you to fix all of this and to get the life I want. O God, I present myself to you. God, above all, I want you, and I want to be faithful to you—whatever you have for me, wherever you lead me.*

Even as I say those things, especially that last sentence, I have to be open to hear my heart say, "John, you are a liar! You don't want God above all else." Even here, we can turn to God, present ourselves to him, and intend to abide in him in light of the recalcitrant parts of the heart. We must recall that "whenever our heart condemns us, God is greater than our heart, and he knows everything" (1 John 3:20).

> *Oh, God, I know parts of my heart do not want you. Parts of my heart do not even want to present itself to you but instead want to stew in worry and seek control. Lord, here I am. I present myself to you again, in the deepest truth of my heart, to be with you in this.*

I may not be able to sustain this intention all day, but this prayer of presenting is within our power any time we become aware of it. This is something you can do right now. What has your heart been turning to today to navigate life's troubles, worries, or frustrations? Can you turn to the Lord in light of those things to put them off and intend to be with him in the truth?

PRACTICE

Prayers of Intention

At the heart of this practice is a retraining of our morning and daily intentions, a kind of prayer of presenting:

> Do not present your members to sin as instruments for unrighteousness, but present yourselves to God as those who have been brought from death to life, and your members to God as instruments for righteousness. For sin will have no dominion over you, since you are not under law but under grace. (Rom. 6:13–14)

> I appeal to you therefore, brothers, by the mercies of God, to present your bodies as a living sacrifice, holy and acceptable to God, which is your spiritual worship. Do not be conformed to this world, but be transformed by the renewal of your mind, that by testing you may discern what is the will of God, what is good and acceptable and perfect. (Rom. 12:1–2)

Prayers of intention will always have a twofold focus: attending to where your heart is actually going and then presenting yourself to God so your intentions can be reoriented around him and his way. These will often be short moments with God throughout your day, beginning right when you wake up, that help reground you in God's reality. In appendix 2, we outline this more fully, but for the sake of beginning, we focus solely on what we call the "Prayer of Presenting." As noted above, in presenting yourself to God, you are *intending* to live life based not on your own internal resources but on your abiding in Christ.

To take on this practice, we suggest you begin your day, every day, with a short exercise to present yourself to God. For this prayer specifically, give yourself about three minutes right when you wake up, as soon as your eyes open. Do this before you go to the bathroom, get a drink of water, or begin your coffee regimen.

First, briefly, attend to where your soul wants to go. Where does your heart want to lead you? What worries, anxieties, fears, joys, and loves reveal themselves? Do not spend too long on this, possibly a minute or less, lest you get caught up in where your heart leads. Notice what you are feeling and thinking, and pay attention to the treasures of your heart.

Second, spend a couple of minutes intentionally presenting yourself to the Lord. Say, "Lord, I am here, I present myself to you. Here I am. I want to be with you today before all the other treasures of my heart." Allow yourself to sit with him—let him be first to you and enjoy the moment. Sometimes you will find enjoyment and peace here, and this is wonderful. Other times your soul may betray you with its old conditioning. Maybe you don't want to present yourself to the Lord or you feel "out of it" or you want to go back to the first movement of your heart upon waking. If so, don't hide it; tell it to God. Tell the Lord, "Yes, Lord, I don't feel like doing this. I feel . . . [tell him what you feel]. This is true of me, Lord, but I am here. And I present myself to you. Oh, God, have mercy. Here I am." You may find new joy emerge in this over time, a brief reprieve from your knee-jerk reactions. Try it. It is within your power to open to the Lord.

Last, consider, just for a moment, what you believe this day holds for you, what meetings you have, plans you've laid out, or troubles you think are coming your way. Pray them in as straightforward a manner as possible:

Lord, here are the thoughts on my heart. Take them, they are
yours. Lord, I am yours. Help me be with you in these things.
Help me abide in you here, and all that this day holds. I want to
be faithful to you in all that you call me into. Here I am. Amen.

You may consider ways to adapt this in other rhythms of your
life, like when you get to work and see the piles on your desk or
the emails in your inbox or the fellow worker you clash with or
the stressful project. Or, perhaps, you might consider adopting a
prayer of intention when you pull in the driveway after a long day
and need a minute to intend to be present with the Lord in your
parenting. For those of us with little kids, sometimes it is taking a
minute longer in the bathroom to intend to parent with patience
when we feel our patience waning. There are endless ways to adapt
the prayer of intention so we engage life in the Lord with actual
intention rather than simply letting our old training and intentions of the flesh determine how we live. Bless you in this practice.

7

Who Am I, Really?
Collecting Our Hearts to Him

In the noise and busyness of this world, we can easily lose focus on who we are, and, more importantly, *whose* we are. As you scroll through social medial feeds, comparing your life with others, do you struggle to focus on who you are in Christ? With all that you take on in your life, does God remain at the center of your identity? The word *recollection* is how we used to talk about keeping God at the center of our lives. To be recollected is to have your heart centered on Christ and who you are in Christ. Even before social media, the internet, and even electricity, we recognized the temptation to allow the busyness of the world, the distractions of our envy, and the comparisons we make to take our eyes off our primary identity in Christ.

I am often tempted to use secondary identities (like professor, author, scholar) as my primary identity. These identities, however, cannot bear the weight of who I am, and particularly who I am in Christ. As I focused on the prayer of recollection over the years, I began to see how these secondary identities want to reign in a way they shouldn't. I want to use them to find security in my life, but no security exists there. In these places, I pray, "Father, these things do not define me. I am yours. I am defined by Christ."

Confronted with all the various ways we fail to remain centered in Christ, we turn to the prayer of recollection. This prayer focuses on recollecting the truth about ourselves so we can walk with God in reality. Philippians 3 provides us with the framework for this prayer, helping us see ways we can use secondary identities as primary identities. Paul leads us to reframe who we are in Christ, showing how everything else finds its proper place only in relation to Christ.

As we witness the ministry and formation of the apostle Paul in the New Testament, it becomes clear that Paul's identity is fixed in Christ. That is how he thinks of himself—he is in Christ Jesus. In Philippians 3, we discover that in the days before Paul's conversion, he used to find his identity in the flesh. He used his works, spirituality, and abilities to ground himself before God and others. He was trying to perfect himself in his own power—that was his Pharisaical life. But in Jesus he has a different way. Now, he can say, "I am not interested in that at all," or, as he explicitly writes,

> But whatever gain I had, I counted as loss for the sake of Christ. Indeed, I count everything as loss because of the surpassing worth of knowing Christ Jesus my Lord. For his sake I have suffered the loss of all things and count them as rubbish, in order that I may gain Christ and be found in him, not having a righteousness of my own that comes from the law, but that which comes through faith in Christ, the righteousness from God that depends on faith. (Phil. 3:7–9)

The very things that used to animate and drive Paul's life he now saw as rubbish in light of Christ. As one redeemed by Jesus, Paul was no longer interested in having a righteousness of his own derived from the law; he now desired the righteousness that comes only from God through faith. However, his former inclinations toward life in his strength and flesh did not disappear from his life immediately upon conversion. And the same is true for us. As our experience reveals, these things continue to tempt our hearts. Recollection, therefore, is the call to ground oneself in the truth of who we are in Christ, and, in doing so, to reframe everything else in the reality of that truth. In light of Christ, Paul saw his former life as self-serving, worldly, and faithless.

Two major movements to the prayer of recollection follow the passage in Philippians. The first is a prayer of detachment, or to use the language of Ephesians 4, of "putting off." The goal here is to name all the things we seek to use for gain *outside of Christ.* These are not necessarily bad in themselves. Paul even includes his zeal on the list! But if we are using any of these to secure ourselves before God, or to ground our deepest identity, then they become works of the flesh.

The second major movement of the prayer of recollection is a prayer of attachment. The goal here is to name the truth of who we are in Christ. This portion parallels the "putting off" aspects of the prayer of detachment by "putting on" the "new man" (see Eph. 4:22–24). The "old man" is not simply the "old self," as some translations have it. The "old man" we put off is who we were in Adam, and our putting on the "new man" is putting on Christ and who we are in Christ. The prayer of recollection guides us in the commands in Scripture to put on Christ and put off the flesh. In doing so, it regrounds us in the truth of who we truly are in Christ Jesus through prayers of detachment and attachment.

The Prayer of Detachment

In the prayer of recollection, we take the truth that Paul narrates and make it a prayer for ourselves. In the first part, we "consider as loss" all the things that tempt us to find our identity outside of Christ. After this, we turn to "consider as loss" all things in comparison to Christ. We are going to detach (at least we are going to speak this detachment to God) from potential idols of the heart. Just because we say we are detached from something, of course, does not make it true. We must not naively think that if we claim to lay these things down, that they are magically put off. Rather, we are naming the objective truth of our life in Christ Jesus and subjectively giving ourselves to this truth. We must be watchful of our hearts in this time, because they will tell us what things are difficult to admit or claim. We may be surprised what our hearts reveal to us. We watch to see what we use to try to establish a firm foundation outside of Christ. If we pay attention, we will discover rather quickly what things are difficult to truly put off.

In the prayer of detachment, we try to internalize where Paul is leading us in Philippians 3. Therefore, we pray,

> Lord, my life is hidden with Christ in you [Col. 3:3], and in him, I am your child [Gal. 4:5]. That is who I am. But in saying that, I'm also reminding myself of who I am not. At my core, I am not a successful person, and I'm not a failure. I'm not a wealthy person or a poor person. I'm not a lawyer, I'm not a teacher, I'm not a mother or a father. Lord, this isn't what I am. Lord, I'm not a student or a professor. These things do not define me, nor do they ground my identity in you.

I (Kyle) remember when John first taught me this prayer. What came as a surprise was when I prayed, "Lord, at my core, I am not a student." I had been a seminary student for several years, having already completed two master's degrees. But as those words came into my mind, I struggled to speak them. I hadn't realized how deeply I was using "student" to ground who I was before God and, even more so, before others. It was not just any kind of student but *seminary* student that I was trying to use to buoy my soul. But it kept going. It wasn't just that I was a seminary student but a good one, a flourishing student. This would continue when I was a PhD student. I wrestled with using each level of education I received as a way to define myself in the presence of God and others, so that when I tried to put them off, my heart held on. Only in praying through this prayer did I come to see how much I didn't want to put these things down. But at my core, this is not who I am in Christ.

It is important to remember that even though we should detach from these identities, that does not mean they are bad. Most of these are good. Yet none of them are enough to make life meaningful. They are not substantial enough to ground our identity. But that won't stop us from trying. Our ultimate grounding in this life is Christ, and in comparison, everything else is rubbish.

When you pray this prayer, therefore, work your way through your various roles in life, such as "I'm not a student." Run through your occupation. Bring your role as a son, a daughter, a father, a mother, or whatever it is before the Lord. But don't stop there. Name traits you may use to ground your life and define yourself. Many of us use traits to define who we are, like "I'm a very loving person," "I'm a kind person," "I'm an angry person," or "I'm an anxious person." Whatever you are using, detach yourself from these things. In detaching from them, you are not leaving them behind; many are good and meaningful callings. You want to simply name the truth that these do not establish you before God. Name these secondary identities to God as a way to reground them on your most fundamental identity in Christ Jesus.

We often fail to realize how deep some of these identities and traits go. We don't recognize how we use them to define us. When this happens, failure becomes particularly undoing. If we lose our job or put all our happiness in being a mother, a pastor, or a success and those unravel, we begin to flail. The only identity that can truly bear the weight of our souls is who we are in Christ. In him, we are fully accepted and fully forgiven. All other attempts to find our identity outside of Christ become weights to the soul, a yoke of our own making that is too heavy to bear. We cannot possibly ground our identity in being a parent, a student, a success, a failure, a teacher, or a preacher. Yet it is easy to try. It becomes even easier when we succeed at these things. The prayer of detachment undermines this by declaring liberation to the soul—these things are not who we are.

I (John) started praying this prayer many years ago, and it became especially important to me whenever I went to preach or teach somewhere. I know I have a desire to please people, to be honored by them, and to be loved by them, so I needed to recollect my heart to God before I taught. Before I would walk on stage, even as I was being introduced, I was praying, "Lord, at the core of me, this does not define me." Sometimes I would resonate with this and find it really meaningful. Other times my heart would reject it.

When we pray this way, it is like sending a sonar signal down into the soul, seeing what kind of response our heart sends back. Sometimes we resonate deeply with it. Other times we speak the truth to our souls and another response comes to the surface. Up from our hearts rises a rejection of the truth, and we hear, "Liar! You don't believe that!" In these moments, we know that we still want to ground our lives in the affirmations of others. The Spirit, who is also in our souls bearing witness to the truth (Rom. 8:16), knows this too, of course. In these places of unbelief, we need to know that the Lord died for us in our sin, even here. This is why we cannot pray the truth merely once but must enter into a lifetime of prayer that recollects our hearts in truth to God.

The Prayer of Attachment

After we "put off" these identities as being unfit to secure ourselves before God, we now turn to "putting on" the truth of who we are in Christ. As a Christian, you are in Christ Jesus, united to him and sharing in his life. And you need to hear the word of Scripture spoken to you: "There is therefore now no condemnation for those who are in Christ Jesus" (Rom. 8:1). Furthermore, because we are in Christ, we have access to the Father (Eph. 2:18). As Christians, we are no longer aliens to the life of God but are members of

God's household (Eph. 2:19–22). We have died with Christ and have, therefore, been raised with him, such that our "life is hidden with Christ in God" (Col. 3:3). We are caught up in Christ such that we share by grace what is Christ's by nature—his Sonship. We are now beloved children of the Father in Christ. This is who we really are. Consider what it would mean if you thought about your life fundamentally as one in union with Christ—no longer condemned but accepted, forgiven, and redeemed. Consider how your life might look different if you embraced that this was your true self and if this was how you prayed.

In the attachment section of this prayer, the goal is to be reoriented to the truth of who you are in Christ Jesus, being honestly open to the question, "Is this how I really feel?" The prayer of attachment, therefore, is something like this: "God, I was created for you. I came into this world in sin and brokenness, longing for perfect love but seeking it in my flesh. Now, in Christ Jesus, I am clothed with Christ's righteousness. That is who I am, one fully pardoned from guilt and shame, and one who is fully accepted by him. In Christ I'm precious and beloved; that's who I am."

As we pray that prayer, our first thought may be, *Thank you, God, that is so good! Thank you!* Others, however, might first think, *Lord, I don't know . . . is that true?* If that is true of you, come out of hiding. If your heart is not there and your mind is elsewhere, do not pause prayer and turn to self-talk. That is the moralist who cannot believe their value comes from outside themselves—from in Christ—and believes they have to achieve this value on their own (even in prayer). In the presence of God, the moralist gives himself a pep talk of the flesh. After he puffs up his flesh, he unpauses prayer to pray, "God, I'm doing what I should be doing, and that's what's really important."

Instead, in the presence of God, we need to come out of hiding. In the presence of God, we need to proclaim the truth to God and seek his mercy. As you pray the prayer of attachment, if you are struggling to affirm it, then tell God, "Lord, even as I'm praying this, I don't experience it as true." Or perhaps, "Father, I don't like this. Here I am. Oh, God, help me. This is why Jesus died for me!" Now you are in his yoke again, and you cannot go wrong there (Matt. 11:28–30).

As you seek to recollect your heart before God, you may once again be reminded of one of our axioms of prayer: prayer is not a place to be good; it is a place to be honest. Do not waste your time in prayer trying to prove to God that you are a good Christian. Rather, rest in full forgiveness and tell Jesus everything. Hold nothing back. When something bothers you, do not pause prayer to have a conversation with yourself. Tell him the truth. Remember that God knows you do not know how to pray as you ought, and he has sent the Spirit to intercede for you by groaning in your soul (Rom. 8:26). The Spirit searches all things and has already explored the deepest depths of your heart. God knows and sees, so open your heart to him.

The Struggle of Recollection

One of the real struggles with putting on Christ is how little we may feel that we have actually put him on. It is odd to put on that "there is therefore now no condemnation for those who are in Christ Jesus" (Rom. 8:1) when you may feel condemned (recall 1 John 3:19–20). Fortunately, our feelings are not certain and clear measures of reality but only show us how our hearts respond to reality. If we don't feel forgiven but feel anxious or condemned, the greatest danger to our souls is to move away from God's presence rather than toward him. This is where our views about how the Christian life progresses can be either helpful or incredibly damaging. If we assume that as mature Christians, we shouldn't feel what we do, then we will try to defeat these things in our flesh—the very things we have no hope of confronting outside of Christ. Rather, we need to put off the flesh and the ways of Adam to embrace the truth that we are clothed in Christ's righteousness.

As we share in Christ's righteousness, we are forgiven, redeemed, and righteous, but that does not mean sin has been eradicated from our lives. As John tells us in 1 John 1:8–10, "If we say we have no sin, we deceive ourselves, and the truth is not in us. If we confess our sins, he is faithful and just to forgive us our sins and to cleanse us from all unrighteousness. If we say we have not sinned, we make him a liar, and his word is not in us." God's salvation does not push us to use our own resources to navigate life independently from him. God's salvation binds us to him so we learn to depend on him for all things, even when we don't feel forgiven or loved by him. Because our righteousness is found outside of ourselves, and because the Son and the Spirit are interceding for us, in us, and through us, we must come to our Father in honesty, telling him what we are feeling and naming the truth of our sin as we are aware of it. Anything less than that is not truly drawing near but is instead a strategy to keep God at arm's length.

Drawing near to God is more than an objective truth we proclaim. To draw near, we seek him personally and with our whole heart. Stopping with the objective truth of our salvation is a failure to follow where Christ truly leads. We are called to live into these realities, knowing by faith that they are true. When we discover we are forgiven in Christ, this should lead us to confess our sins. Forgiveness cannot merely be an idea—that is not to grasp it at all—we need to live into it. To embrace that we are forgiven is to come out of hiding to explore and confess the deep truths of our hearts. Simply affirming the truth of these things is a failure to understand what Scripture calls us to. The objective reality of who we are in Christ establishes the journey we are called to, just as the objective reality of being named husband and wife should lead to mutual self-giving in love. The objective truth creates the context and conditions to give ourselves deeply to this process of putting off and putting on, so that we can name the truth of our subjective experience to the God who offers himself to us in love.

The struggle we discover in the prayer of recollection, then, is threefold.

First, we struggle to lay down what we use to ground our identity before God, ourselves, and others. People who link their identity with their calling often struggle most deeply with this. Pastors, for instance, can be tempted to use their role as "pastor" to secure a standing before God and others. But before the face of God, no security exists outside of Christ. We must seek the Father in Christ. A second struggle exists as well, however, which is trying to "put off" the old man by reading through the detachment portion of this prayer. We may find our hearts are not really present to the putting off section. Instead of willfully putting off the flesh, we may be trying to be good at praying this prayer. Of course, this is also a temptation with the putting on portion. The antidote is to talk honestly with God about what is really going on within you.

This leads to the third struggle, which is to seek out sight rather than faith. When we put on the truth of who we are in Christ, it is easy to naively think we will experience an immediate change. We love the instantaneous, but we struggle with the process. We don't want to navigate the remaining sin and brokenness we have before God; we want him to make them disappear. This is the desire to want to bear fruit without having to abide. We should not despair of our failings but know it is good news that we can do nothing without him (John 15:5).

To pray prayers in faith, we name the truth of who we are in Christ Jesus and lay aside all the ways our commonsensical views tell us to find power, meaning, and flourishing in the autonomy of the flesh. In faith, we come out of hiding and tell God the truth about how we are tempted by our flesh. As we pray in faith, we must attend to our desire for sight and how it betrays us. Our eyes tell us things different from Scripture about how the world works. Scripture tells us that our lives are hidden with Christ in God (Col. 3:3), but we look around and wonder, *What does that even mean? My life doesn't look hidden with Christ in God.*

We may be reading 2 Corinthians 5:17, which says, "Therefore, if anyone is in Christ, he is a new creation. The old has passed away; behold, the new has come," and wonder, *Am I really new? The old hasn't seemed to have passed away. I still see a lot of sin.* Suddenly we may think it is better to live in fantasy by fooling ourselves into thinking that all is fine. Sadly, fantasy and self-deception are sometimes easier to embrace than the reality of God's kingdom, because reality may not make a lot of sense. This is where we are called ever-deeper into reality—into the truth about ourselves as well as the truth about what God has done—because by faith we trust that God defines these realities. To pray in faith is to grasp ahold of God for understanding and experiencing all these complex, contradictory realities within. Because he is the only hope we truly have in this world.

PRACTICE

Prayers of Recollection

For the prayer of recollection, set aside twenty to thirty minutes for prayer and meditation. This may be a practice you consider doing weekly, at a set time, or as part of another practice.

First, begin with a simple prayer of intention (specifically, the prayer of presenting) by offering your heart to God and acknowl-edging your intention to be with him, learn from him, and rest in him. Don't move from this too quickly, as if it were just a transition to more important things. Pause here with the Lord. "Lord, I'm here. I'm presenting myself to you. I am yours" (Rom. 6:13). Be open to the truth of what is going on within. If your heart truly wants to present itself to God, wonderful. If you feel resistance or boredom, tell the Lord and be with him in the truth of these feelings. He already knows.

Second, ask the Lord to unveil the realities of your heart and life that you need to put off. The focus of this prayer, as we have presented it, is on identities we may grab on to, but be open to whatever the Lord may illumine in your heart and your life. Consider ways you try to use identities other than who you are in Christ as a firm foundation for who you are before God and others. Lay down any potential idols of your heart. Consider as loss all of these things compared to Christ (Phil. 3:7–8).

> *Prayer of detachment:* Father, at my core, in the depths of my spirit, I am not a success or a failure, a wealthy person or a poor person, someone who needs to be honored, or a good person or a bad person. At my core, my identity is not being a good or a bad mother or father, friend, or churchgoer. I am not a kind person or an angry person. I am not a worker, a professional, a professor, a teacher, a preacher. I am not a _____ [fill in with your life and confess and lay down any idolatries of your heart]. [Again, if your soul is rightly engaged in this, rejoice. If your soul is bored or does not want to do this, tell God—tell God all that you are feeling. Acknowledge your need for him.]

Third, speak the truth of who you are in Christ to your soul and attend to how your soul responds. In Christ, there is now no condemnation. In Christ, you are a child of the Father. In Christ, you know forgiveness, redemption, and reconciliation. In Christ, you have access to the Father. Your identity in Christ is your true self. You are not defined from within but from without—in Christ Jesus. You are not accepted because you have crafted a beautiful life; you are received as beautiful because he loves you (Phil. 3:9–11).

Prayer of attachment: I was created for union with God. Lord, I came into the world in sin, but I long for perfect love. In your grace, I have now been clothed with Christ's righteousness, with full pardon from guilt and full acceptance from God. I am now precious in God's eyes. God calls me his beloved. That is who I truly am. [Confess any unbelief in your heart.]

At this point, resolve to keep your heart and mind attentive to the Lord and who you are in him. You may feel the need to pray, "I believe; help my unbelief!" (Mark 9:24). In this place, your heart may have all sorts of expectations, and, at times, they may be met, while much of the time they won't be. Bring this to the Lord. "Lord, I don't know where you are. I feel alone here. But here I am, I am yours." Open to the truth of your need for him. Be recollected to Christ in weakness to know the power of God (2 Cor. 12:9–10).

Then, it may prove fruitful to meditate on a couple of passages about who you are in Christ Jesus. Prayerfully read the following and use them to open to the truth of who you are in the Lord.

For our sake he made him to be sin who knew no sin, so that in him we might become the righteousness of God. (2 Cor. 5:21)

Indeed, I count everything as loss because of the surpassing worth of knowing Christ Jesus my Lord. For his sake I have suffered the loss of all things and count them as rubbish, in order that I may gain Christ and be found in him, not having a righteousness of my own that comes from the law, but that which comes through faith in Christ, the righteousness from God that depends on faith—that I may know him and the power of his resurrection, and may share his sufferings, becoming like him in his death, that by any means possible I may attain the resurrection from the dead. (Phil. 3:8–11)

Abide in me, and I in you. As the branch cannot bear fruit by itself, unless it abides in the vine, neither can you, unless you abide in me. I am the vine; you are the branches. Whoever abides in me and I in him, he it is that bears much fruit, for apart from me you can do nothing. (John 15:4–5)

Hold open your life to God. Know that it is *in him* that we become the righteousness of God. If your heart is cold to these texts, tell God. This once again establishes in experience that God is greater than our hearts (1 John 3:20).

8

Being Watchful

I iving in the chaos-reigning dorms in college and then experiencing life with roommates for several years after, I (Kyle)
ong time in perpetual noise. When I decided to go back
nary, I ended up living alone—with no internet and no
on—and the silence and solitude were reorienting. I could
ny body and soul that I needed time and space to reorder
, and the noise, chaos, and busyness had not allowed for it
In all the distraction and clatter, I was missing what was
ning in my heart. I had not thought much about prayers of
on, so I allowed my seminary training to dictate my inten-
I was intent on getting good grades, so I did whatever my
sors told me. I was not recollected or grounded in who I was
rist but was tossed to and fro by the various identities and
I played. I was also failing to collect the everyday realities of
fe with the Lord. I was living an unexamined life before God.
no idea how much I was missing.

he importance of reflection and examination, I came to dis-
r, was at the heart of the original Protestant vision of the Chris-
life. Closer to our own context, examination was a central

141

feature of Puritan and early evangelical understandings of life with God.[1] We are to know ourselves, not for self-knowledge alone but to know the full extent of what the Lord has saved us from. But the human heart is deceitful (Jer. 17:9) and, in particular, self-deceptive. We do not simply deceive others—we deceive ourselves. Because we are often not honest with ourselves about our motives, desires, and character, we have long been encouraged to set aside time in the evening for self-examination.[2] This prayer of examine requires a watchfulness of heart and life, not for their own sakes but so we offer our lives to the Lord in full. This is a prayer where we allow our lives to speak.

Self-examination feels difficult because we are tempted to look at ourselves outside of Christ. As Martin Luther declared, "If Christ is put aside and I look only at myself, then I am done for."[3] This is the experience many of us have. Self-examination feels like the opposite of the freedom we are supposed to know in Christ. Christian self-examination, however, is not something we are called to outside of Christ. What makes self-examination possible is the objective truth that, as Christians, we are in him.

Our goal in self-examination is to see the depths of our depravity, sin, and misordered desire, not in themselves but in light of Christ. We needn't fear what we find in ourselves, however much we might struggle with this, because there is no condemnation for us in Christ Jesus (Rom. 8:1). Recognizing the depth of our sin and brokenness allows us to embrace God more deeply. When we rest in the truth that there is no condemnation in Christ, we have the assurance that allows us to navigate our brokenness. While our hearts can be messy and disorienting, our lives confront us with a mirror to see our hopes, fears, failures, and joys. In the prayer of examine, we collect these moments of our lives to bring to God.

Because we are in Christ, our lives provide the fodder for our prayers.

Because we are his, we can see every moment as an opportunity to offer ourselves to him.

Because the Spirit groans within us, we groan too, holding our lives open to the One who sees and knows.

The prayer of examine is built on the belief that if we pay attention to our lives, every moment is an opportunity to learn unceasing prayer (1 Thess. 5:17). This prayer is an examination of one of our most precious commodities: our time. If we do not set aside time to intentionally consider, moment by moment, our days and weeks, then much of our lives will go by unnoticed. Like the person who is shocked by how many hours of screen time they use, if we do not examine our lives, we won't know the truth.

I remember sitting on my couch at the end of the day, my children just tucked into bed. I opened my life to the Lord and considered my day. Hour by hour, through conversations, emotions, deadlines, joys, and frustrations, I offered my day to the Lord. Then, to my surprise, all of the moments I normally would have forgotten flooded my consciousness. Many of these were little things—a note from a thankful student, a laugh with a colleague, a precious moment with my children—but they were good. My heart was filled with thankfulness for the Lord's kindness. I stopped and wondered how often I let these pieces of goodness slip by in my forgetfulness. I considered how little I tended to thank God and how forgetful I really am.

As with several of the prayers we have addressed, including praying the Psalms and the Lord's Prayer, there is a danger, on the one hand, of speaking words that do not truly open your heart to God or, on the other hand, of turning inward and merely talking to yourself. This is where examination (or, sometimes, *examen*) is such an important practice.[4] With a prayer of examine, there will be a temptation (and, at first, probably a tendency) to simply think about your life. While that may be necessary to get used to the practice, it is by no means the desired goal. The goal of examination is never self-knowledge for its own sake. There is nothing distinctively Christian about knowing yourself. Rather, the goal is to know yourself in such a way that leads you to embrace God in truth. The goal is to examine your life *with God*, to know and explore your life in the context of God's presence and grace.

There is, however, a deeper reason why the practice of examination was so important for our foremothers and forefathers in the faith. It was a key aspect of training their hearts for watchfulness. Peter commands us, in general, to "be watchful" (1 Pet. 5:8). Furthermore, as Paul admonishes, "Continue steadfastly in prayer, being watchful in it with thanksgiving" (Col. 4:2). We are called to "be watchful" in prayer. It is easier not to be watchful. It is easier to pray through a list, an agenda, or our desires and wants and get it over with. Watchfulness requires our patient attending to our experience in God's presence. Watchfulness is the posture of the heart that seeks God honestly in reality and not fantasy. But being watchful in prayer cannot be turned on like a switch. It stems from a heart not merely attuned to one's own agenda but attuned to itself and God in truth. Even more so, being watchful is meant not only for prayer but for all of life.

One important place to be watchful is in our self-talk. When we pause prayer and begin talking to ourselves, we need to carefully consider what we say and what we turn to. Our self-talk is a window into our souls, and it unveils the deep beliefs and desires of our hearts. But it is not only what we say in prayer but also what we don't say that we need to watch over. We must consider what parts of our lives we don't bring to God—what longings, desires, and fantasies we withhold from him.

Our church went through a season when we focused on lament because we realized we didn't know how to lament well. Those of us at the church had grown up in an evangelicalism that never emphasized lament as a central feature of prayer. After several years, we realized that recovering a lost emphasis led to losing others. We became less exuberant in our praise. We failed to carve out space for thankfulness. Our prayers became so focused on what was wrong that we failed to bring to the Lord what was right. It took a corporate watchfulness of our prayers to help us see what kinds of things we didn't bring to the Lord.

What kinds of things pass by that you do not attend to? Are you watchful over your life, or do the moments, emotions, and days simply fade? Have you forgotten thankfulness? Do you seek God in your work and ask him what he is doing through it? Are there certain emotions or reactions—anger, envy, frustration, or worry—that you aren't watchful over? Do you engage these outside of Christ or with Christ? Are these emotions only for you, or are they for the Lord who forgives and loves?

As you consider all that you give yourself to in life (relationships, family, emotions, loves, joys, and freedoms), are those places where God is known and sought? I once shared a story with a friend about a difficult part of my work. He asked, "How do you think God sees this situation?" I was dumbstruck. I realized that I never considered or sought God in light of relational difficulties. I thought these difficulties were just for me and were things I was supposed to "solve." I had not paid attention to the relational difficulties in my life and how I responded. In examination, we allow our lives to provide us the content for our prayers. We need to examine both what we give ourselves to, as well as what we fail to—things like thankfulness, forgiveness, or maybe just peace. We need to pray, "Lord, help me be watchful and see all I should be thankful for" (or forgiven of, etc.).

Being Known

In 1 Corinthians 13:12, we are told, "For now we see in a mirror dimly, but then face to face. Now I know in part; then I shall know fully, even as I have been fully known." In this age of faith, we see in a mirror dimly. In eternity, however, we will see God face-to-face. In that day of face-to-face intimacy with God, we will know as we have been known. Notice how our knowing God is connected to our being known by him. Jesus has called us to himself, not merely to do what he told us to but to be known by him as we come to know him. Our knowledge of God and our knowledge of ourselves are deeply intertwined realities. To know God entails, Paul tells us, that we are those who have come to be *known by him* (Gal. 4:9).

To know as we have been known requires that we open our hearts and lives to God and not only to ourselves (although this must also be true). We are not like the child who has to tell her parents something she did that she is deeply ashamed about. We may have things we are deeply ashamed about, but God already knows! God knows even when we are ignoring these things, ignoring the truth, and trying to pray "rightly." He calls us to know his forgiveness, his mercy, and his grace in the actual reality of our lives. Examination is what makes these things known to us.

In examination, we look through our days to see what our lives proclaim to be true. How we allocate our time, what gets us frustrated, how we spend money, and what takes place in our interactions are all held before God. In examination, we follow the command to "consider your ways" (Hag. 1:7). I may see that while I think of myself as stingy with time, I am actually generous with it to others. I may realize that I am not the cheerful giver I like to think I am. I might see how time spent grumbling caused me to miss the goodness lavished on me. Examination regrounds us in the Lord in the reality of our lives, that we might hold "every thought captive" to him (2 Cor. 10:5). Examination considers our daydreams, fantasies, and the things we covet so that we can hold open our longings before the Lord and seek him as our good.

In the practice of examination, Psalm 139 is often a helpful starting point. There David prays,

> Search me, God, and know my heart;
> test me and know my anxious thoughts.

> See if there is any offensive way in me,
>   and lead me in the way everlasting. (vv. 23–24 NIV)

David desires to be known by God, to see any offensive way in his life, and to know all his anxious thoughts. No matter how you pray a prayer of examine, it will follow this instinct. This prayer is a place for you to make your life known to God, who already sees and knows. Take seriously that your life is a picture of where your heart truly is, and see how much of your life you miss completely.

Praying the Prayer of Examine

We will turn to more practical guidance in the practice section following this chapter, but before we do so, it is helpful to recall that the structure isn't an end in itself. It is important scaffolding for a while, just as training wheels are necessary to help a child who is learning how to ride a bike. The goal is to no longer need them so they can fly forward in the joy and freedom of riding. This is also true regarding whatever structure one chooses for praying a prayer of examine. But unlike using training wheels after learning to ride a bike, at times we must go back to the structure to help us enter into parts of our lives that seem to disappear from our attention. This can happen in examination, as the old habits of denial lead us away from the very things we should be bringing to the Lord.

Throughout the generations, many have made use of a prayer of examine. Often someone considers their life every evening (or in an extended time taken away from "normal" life). This needn't be more than twenty to thirty minutes, and it is a time to consider what has happened that day, or, if at the end of the week, during the week that has passed. In the evening, one might, for instance, recall the beginning of the day and simply work through as much as they can recall—hour by hour—pausing on emotions, events, or even people for the sake of prayer.

We may want to highlight specific aspects of our lives with God. Some find that looking for moments of thankfulness is particularly important when examining their lives. Others may attend to events in their day and ask the Lord for guidance about what they did or did not do. "Lord, what were you calling me into in that circumstance?" For others still, what emerges in their examination are particular sins to consider with the Lord. Focusing on relational interactions, good or bad, and emotions regarding those can be particularly telling. Here we wrestle through the truth of our hearts and our calling to love our neighbors as ourselves.

As we walk through our days, trying to be attentive to God, we ask the Lord to search us and know us. Over time we increasingly recognize the themes in our lives. We may begin to see that we are not really open to others, so we bring that in prayer: "Lord, my heart isn't open to these people. I have not loved my neighbor as myself. Help me open my heart to them in love. What does it look like to be open to them even here and now?" We may see that we have allowed many of our days and our interactions to go by without really attending to others. We may become aware that we don't care about this right now and that we are cold to this process. Tell that to God: "Lord, as I look at my day, I don't even seem to care right now. My heart seems so hard! Oh, God, have mercy." Be open to where that honesty leads. We cannot dictate where the cold heart will go if it is honest with God. That, perhaps, is God's business as he prays within us by the Spirit (Rom. 8:26) and as we cry out, "Abba! Father!" (Rom. 8:15).

When I (Kyle) regularly practice examination, several things happen. First, I tend to pray more for others. I often recall a conversation with someone I normally would have forgotten, where it was clear that this person needed prayer. So I pray. Sometimes I recall that I told them I would pray for them, and normally I would have forgotten, but now I have the space ready to bring them to the Lord.

Second, I find that I am more thankful. Prayers of examine help me attend to little things—an encouraging text from my spouse or a friend, a meaningful conversation, or a short space of peace in the midst of an abnormally busy day. As I pray through my thankfulness, I am more in touch with it and can experience and sit with a thankful heart. As I do so, thankfulness bubbles up through me to God.

Third, I become more aware of themes in my life and patterns in my behavior. Whether it is thankfulness, prayerlessness, hopelessness, or even just a desire not for rest but for escape, I discover I am more aware of how these things shape my life. I recognize more and more how they govern and guide my decisions.

A Life Examined

When the prayer of examine becomes a regular rhythm of my life, I tend to leave behind the emphasis on an hour-by-hour overview of my day. That is something I really like about this prayer. Because it helps train the heart to attend and be watchful, I find that I come into this time already holding various things I've collected throughout the day. This space becomes the place where I enter more deeply into what is going on in life rather than simply offering a quick prayer for God to "fix it." I am sometimes tempted to think that God will heal my anger in the same way he healed the blind man's blindness, but he tends not to heal our souls like he heals our bodies. Instead, he calls us to abide precisely in our brokenness so we can learn that his grace is sufficient for us (2 Cor. 12:9). Instead of missing the Lord's shepherding in these matters, I am more open to how these realities are part of my training in humility and dependence. In a strange sort of turnaround, knowledge of our vices and sins becomes a door into knowing his power in my weakness and knowing his mercy and love.[5]

One such experience was when I was attacked by a Christian spreading lies about me online. Against my better judgment, I tried to defend myself, but it quickly digressed into him twisting my words, making up accusations, and trying to paint me in the worst possible light. I immediately had the thought that this was something I needed to bring before God. As I sat in prayer, I spent some time asking the Lord to search my heart.

Lord, search me and know me. I am angry. I am frustrated. I am tired of this coming from people who claim to be Christians yet spread deceit, division, and discord. But there is more. There is a desire in my heart to defeat this person. There is a desire not to defend myself but to somehow publicly expose him so everyone will know he is a liar. But Lord, this isn't mine to defend. This is yours. Lord, I am yours.

When insulted, I turned to my heart and discovered that this same evil lurked in me. I, too, desired to defeat others rather than pray for them.

The frustration and anger that brought me into prayer suddenly led me in a different direction. My prayer needed to be truthful about what I was feeling, but it also needed conditioning: "Lord, forgive as I have forgiven." My examination helped me recall how the Lord's Prayer should condition my praying. This led me to seek God's grace and mercy so that I, too, could flow forth in grace and mercy. A prayer that started in anger became a discussion with the Lord about how I could be open to pray for this person. I didn't know this man or his struggles. I didn't know what the Lord was doing in his life. I didn't know what was driving his rage or why lying about me was somehow fulfilling something in his life. This wasn't mine to know. I prayed, "Lord, have mercy on this person. Meet him in his rage. Meet him in whatever fears and anxieties lead him to disparage me and others." I had to enter into this kind of forgiveness so I could bless even when I was cursed.

While prayers of examine may have a general rhythm to them—walking through our days with the Lord to consider our lives in his presence—they can also become times to sit and deeply consider something too significant to ignore. This does not have to be something bad; it could be something of great joy you still have a divided heart over. The prayer of examine is a deep excavation of one's life with God, regardless of what comes to the surface. If one practices examination daily, then it becomes a rhythm of opening one's life to God to learn to "pray without ceasing" in the midst of all we are experiencing. If this prayer is a weekly practice, it will take on a different form. When this is the case, it will usually be based not on a moment-by-moment examination with God but on larger themes in one's life. Jonathan Edwards thought both forms were necessary, so he encouraged a young Christian with the following:

> Under special difficulties, or when in great need of (or great longings after) any particular mercies for your self or others, set apart a day of secret fasting and prayer alone; and let the day be spent not only in petitions for the mercies you desired, but in searching your heart, and looking over your past life, and confessing your sins before God (not as is wont to be done in public prayer), but by a very particular rehearsal before God, of the sins of your past life from your childhood hitherto, before and after conversion, with particular circumstances and aggravations, also very particularly and fully as possible, spreading all the abominations of your heart before him.[6]

In this sense, Edwards sees the importance of taking special times—lengthier and more involved times—to unpack one's life with God. While some Christians believe that since God forgets our sins, separating them as far as the east is from the west, then we should as well. But Edwards would disagree. We need to recall these sins precisely because God forgets them. We don't dwell on them to beat ourselves up or to somehow live in the past. We recall them so we can consider more deeply what God has done for us, how he forgives and loves us in the present, and how these past sins or experiences continue to form us even to this day. We don't examine our sins in themselves; we examine our lives and our sins as those in Christ. Our goal is to live in reality with God, who calls us to live with him in all things. The prayer of examine is central, therefore, in fostering a watchfulness of heart as we seek to faithfully present ourselves to God as those who can do nothing without him (John 15:5).

PRACTICE

Prayers of Examine

A prayer of examine can be something you practice semi-regularly (i.e., weekly or monthly) or something you practice daily. For the sake of simplicity, we will focus on practicing daily. First, choose a time that will work well for you. For me (Kyle), the time that makes the most sense in my day is right after I put my kids to bed. There is a sense that I am now free, for maybe the first time that day, to do whatever I want to do! This is important. Before I read a book or watch something on TV or unpack my day with my wife, I want to stop for twenty minutes and examine what has really been going on in my day. If I wait much longer, I won't be able to stay awake.

When picking a time, make sure to take the overall rhythm of your life into consideration. You may also want to consider pairing this practice with praying a psalm. This might be a good way to reorient your heart to the Lord in the midst of what is going on in your life. After you have prayed a psalm (if you choose to) or quieted your heart, consider what went on in your day. Unless something immediately jumps out at you, begin by attending to each phase of your day—what happened, how you responded, conversations you had, joys, frustrations, and anything else that took place. Consider what gifts you received that day. What are you thankful for that happened throughout the day? Often I discover many little things helped me rest in the joy of God's providing. Consider your openness to God and others throughout your day. Were you open to what the Lord may have been leading you into? How did you respond to others? What were your intentions as you worked, served, ministered, rested, etc.? How did the previous training of your heart lead you to or away from abiding in Christ?

As you consider your day, pay attention specifically to your desires, longings, self-talk, and emotional reactions: What grabbed your heart today? These are little glimpses into your soul that are necessary to open to God in truth. Examine what was going on in your heart—not apart from the Lord but with him. "Lord, look at my envy. Why do I envy others like I do? Lord, do you see this worry? Look at how quickly I try to worry my way into controlling my life instead of seeking you. Lord, have mercy. Lord, I am so anxious. Help me know your peace in this place." Many of these emotions will be tied to people in your life—people you love, people you might find frustrating, or even people you wish weren't in your life. We will address intercession in the next chapter, but here, hold this person up to the Lord. What comes up in your heart when you relate to this person? Anger? Fear? Frustration? Anxiety? Joy? Love? Peace? Why? "Lord, how am I called to love this person? What might it look like to be at peace with this person? How do I enter into life with them?"

Finally, keep in mind that some (maybe most!) days or evenings, you may not feel like doing this at all. Our suggestion is not to repress that feeling and do it anyway. That may be fine for a while, but it will lead to a repressed prayer life, which feels more unreal and boring over time until you pray less and less. Rather, notice the internal resistance and share this with the Lord. Let this lead you into the prayer of examine as the first thing to examine!

9

Seeing Ourselves and Others in the Love of God

What happens when you try to intercede for someone? Think about the difference between interceding for someone who is really close to you, whose life is deeply interwoven with your life, and someone you barely know. What is your goal in this time with the Lord? For many, intercession is a form of prayer we assume but rarely, if ever, talk about. Unlike other forms of prayer, it seems easy and obvious. *Don't we just ask God to help?*

Intercession, like other modes of prayer, can quickly become compromised and used as a prayer of magic. We can assume if we say the right thing in the right way, then we have embraced the call to pray for one another (1 Tim. 2:1). But prayer is not simply an act we do to achieve our purposes. Prayer is being with God. Prayer is a bold ascent to the throne of grace, where we seek the Father in the Son by the Spirit. Prayer is intentionally entering God's presence, and yet, as we have seen, our prayers can become ways to be absent to God. In intercession specifically, we discover that it is difficult to be present.

The Art of Being Present

In 1975, Edward Tronick and his team did an experiment that became known as the "Still Face Experiment." The video is widely used, though many find it difficult to watch. In the video we see a mother with her year-old baby, playing and smiling and laughing at each other. The mother talks to her baby and the baby responds in her own babble, in a dance of mutual presence where each is mirroring what the other is experiencing. The baby is delighted in her mother and that she is responding to her exuberance in kind. All of a sudden, in the midst of the mother's baby talk, she turns away for a moment and then turns back, completely still-faced. Immediately you can see a change in the baby. *Is this some kind of game?* She starts to smile at her mother, pointing at things and babbling, looking for her mother to respond. Reaching forward, the baby holds both hands up and makes a more troubled noise, clapping at her mother to try to get her attention. But her mother gives no response. The baby screeches and starts moving her body around, trying to break free from the constraints of her high chair. Then she starts crying and turning her face away from her mother.[1]

We are born with the longing to be seen and known. Yet we know what it is like not to be seen, and we know what it is like when others are not really present to us. We know that baby's experience when we share our hearts with someone and come to see, clearly, that they are not really with us. They do not mirror our experience, and as we share ourselves with them, they respond with something completely contrary, abrasive, or simply out of touch. We know the other side of this as well. We can recall times when someone was sharing their heart with us and we realized that our hearts had wandered to something else and we were not present.

Every deep relationship, whether it is a marriage, a parent-child relationship, or a friendship, needs presence. Relationships thrive in presence, but being present is much more than physical proximity. Just as that baby knew she needed her mother to not merely be near her but to be *with* her, we were created to be seen and known in love and to reciprocate by seeing and knowing others in love.

We can't really be present if we do not believe we are seen and known in love. If we are seen and known and not loved, that taps into some of our deepest fears about ourselves. That fear often gives rise to a counterfeit presence. We try to be seen, known, and loved—not in truth but in fantasy. We project an image or avatar at others, representing who we wish we were. Deep down we know this is not who we really are, so we cannot receive love in that place. But God has made himself present in the deepest and most profound ways possible, and he calls us to be present to him so we can be present to others.

I (Kyle) have found this to be difficult, especially in prayer. Sometimes I care only about what I am praying for and see nothing else. I am present to my request but not really to God. Sometimes the opposite is the case! Take, for instance, when I am online scrolling through a social media feed and see a prayer request for someone. I immediately feel guilty for ignoring (or just wanting to ignore) it. As I am scrolling past the request, I make sure to say a quick prayer, often without a name and without explicitly referencing the situation: "Er, Lord, help that person. . . ." In that moment, my goal is not about praying for them; it is simply an attempt to stop feeling guilty.

I am not with these people in prayer. I haven't even tried to internalize their plight. Rather, I am lobbing prayers at God for someone who is far from my heart. Like the still-faced mother with her baby, I am not actually present to this brother or sister in Christ. This kind of intercession contains a threefold absence: 1) I am absent from the person I am praying for, as I name requests to mark off a list; 2) I am absent from myself, since I am not actually entering into the heart of the request; and 3) I am absent from God, because I am not with him with these requests. I'm just lofting them at him. This is the real danger.

Up until now, our focus has been on personal prayer and being with God. Our final form of prayer opens up another avenue in our life in Christ. What does it mean to love our neighbor as ourselves *in prayer*? We are now asking God to do something on behalf of another. Over the past several years when speaking on prayer in churches and at conferences, I've noticed that people tend to divorce intercession from the way of prayer we have been outlining. Intercession, for these folks, seems easier and more simplistic. I sense that the people I talk to have all sorts of questions about why prayer is so difficult, *except for intercession*. Intercession seems like the one obvious mode of prayer. What could be simpler than asking God for good things for others? Just do it! What more could be said?

The sense that intercession is obvious, even if we find it difficult to do (or difficult to remember to do), points to our failure to focus on what is really going on within us when we pray. Praying for someone in Christ requires us to be present in three key ways.

1. To intercede for another, I need to be present to the person I am praying for. I need to be with them in prayer, which means I have to be open to the difficulties or joys they are experiencing.

2. I need to be present to myself *and* my relation to them. Intercession requires that I am with this person, which means I have to be open to how I relate to them. It turns out that intercession awakens the brokenness, pain, and control in our relationships with others.

3. Finally, I need to be present to God who is with me and them in all of this. Intercession is not merely being with another; it is being with them in the presence of God as a way to bring them to the Father.

Without this threefold presence, we cannot fully enter into the calling of intercession. Without being present to God, what we are doing is more akin to offering "good thoughts" on someone's behalf. This is often the reality of praying through a list. It can easily degrade into its secular counterpart: sending *thoughts* and prayers. Without being present to myself, I remain ignorant of how my thoughts and feelings govern and, at times, warp my prayers for others. Without being present to them, I am treating them not as a brother or a sister in Christ but as someone detached from my life. Interceding in Christ, by the Spirit who unites us in him, is a much more profound calling.

Being Present to Another with God

For much of my Christian life, the word *absence* would best define my prayers. I often felt like that baby did before her still-faced mother when I prayed. I wondered why God seemed still-faced and absent to me, when in reality I was the one failing to be present. I needed to intentionally draw near to him, the one who was already with me, and come to trust his presence by faith. Our God is not still-faced before our plight; instead, he is with us, internal to us, in our struggle. With intercession, however, there is another sort of drawing near we must attend to. When we intercede, we are drawing near to another person for whom we are praying, to draw near to God with them. Maybe we hear of a family who are friends of friends and have been struck by a tragedy, so we pray for them. We do not know them personally and are not immediately pulled into their tragedy. Nonetheless, we can personally enter into their circumstances. We can still be *with* them in prayer, if we enter into their tragedy in the Lord.

The danger here is that this can quickly become a Hallmark moment that sounds nice but has no real meaning behind it. But being present to another in the Lord is vastly different from sending thoughts to someone. What we find in Scripture provides us with a more compelling reality. Consider Paul's presence to his churches even when he wasn't able to be with them in person and how this can serve as a model for our own intercession:

> For I want you to know how great a struggle I have for you and for those at Laodicea and for all who have not seen me face to face, that their hearts may be encouraged, being knit together in love, to reach all the riches of full assurance of understanding and the knowledge of God's mystery, which is Christ, in whom are hidden all the treasures of wisdom and knowledge. I say this in order that no one may delude you with plausible arguments. For though I am absent in body, yet I am with you in spirit, rejoicing to see your good order and the firmness of your faith in Christ. Therefore, as you received Christ Jesus the Lord, so walk in him, rooted and built up in him and established in the faith, just as you were taught, abounding in thanksgiving. (Col. 2:1–7)

As a member of Christ, Paul can be present in the Spirit to believers he is not *physically* present to.[2] How might we be present to a brother or sister in the Spirit even though we are physically absent from them? What does this look like for our intercession? What might it look like if we entered into the plight of others and gave ourselves to them in their hurt, joy, sorrow, excitement, and lament? Open your heart and try. If you are praying and you don't feel like you really care, then share that first and ask God to give you a heart that cares. God already knows the truth, so begin with the truth.

Our calling to intercede and be present to one another stems from the truth that the Christian life is a communal reality. As Christians, we are adopted; therefore, we are brought into a new family (Eph. 2:18–19). We have brothers and sisters, even if we have never met them. And as God calls us to himself, he calls us to our brothers and sisters to be "knit together in love." This is why Jesus prays to the Father that we may be one, as he and the Father are one, that the world would know we are loved by the Father (John 17:20–23). Intercession is one way we enter into this reality. To embrace that we are one is to accept the call to be bound together in love (Col. 3:14).

The unity we know in Christ is an aspect of our Christian identity that is easy to ignore in our current context. Yet this is how Scripture understands life within the body of Christ. Paul writes effusively to his brothers and sisters at Corinth: "We have spoken freely to you, Corinthians; our heart is wide open. You are not restricted by us, but you are restricted in your own affections. In return (I speak as to children) widen your hearts also" (2 Cor. 6:11–13). Paul continues to plead with them: "Make room in your hearts for us" (2 Cor. 7:2).

The church at Corinth had become "restricted" by their affections. The way love had formed in their hearts had bound them, so they were unable to open themselves to Paul and, presumably, to others. Paul's response is telling. He pleaded with them to widen (or enlarge) their hearts to receive him and then asked more explicitly, "Make room in your hearts for us." Paul claimed he was talking to them as one talks to a child. This is, of course, exactly how we talk to children! "Will you just love your sister?! Can't you just love your brother?!" As a parent, one of the odder commands you will bark at your child is the command to love. What Paul was pointing to reveals a fundamental aspect of the Christian life necessary for intercessory prayer. We need to enlarge our hearts to and make room for one another. In the act of intercession, we are not praying for those who are far from us, regardless of the physical distance between us. In intercession, we are able to be with one another, because in Christ we really are.

The truth of who we are in Christ and what kind of closeness is available in the Spirit confronts the belief that prayer isn't very meaningful. Few people would verbalize this, but many of us feel it. Prayer can seem like the literal sense of "the least I can do." When tragedy strikes and we pray, sometimes it feels like the smallest possible gesture. But intercession is no mere gesture. Intercession is a prayer of faith, and we are present to another to carry them, in the Spirit, to the Father. Intercession is trusting that in the Spirit we can be present to this person and their circumstances. We can lift them up to the Lord. Maybe more profoundly, we know by faith that we are not alone in this. We are with them in the intercession of the Son and the Spirit and are partaking of their praying. This is not merely a nice idea; it is the bold ascent to the throne of grace in the prayers of faith. Far from "the least I can do," intercession grasps ahold of the spiritual realities of being in Christ with our brothers and sisters.

Present to Oneself with God

It is important to be present to what is going on in our own hearts as we hold people before the Father, making ourselves one with their plight. It may at times be difficult to be present to others. I (Kyle) find it difficult to enter into someone else's joy when I am not feeling joyful or when their joy represents an unfulfilled longing of my heart. I can experience envy when I pray for them and see how that envy influences how I pray for them. It is easy to pray, "God, protect them in this season with this money they've inherited. I worry they will spend it foolishly." While that might not be a bad request, it may stem from my own envy rather than from reality. Deep down I am really thinking, *I would do something more meaningful with that money than they would. I should have been the person to get it.*[3]

The same can be true as I intercede for those in pain. In my joy, I might struggle to be present to them in their pain, just as in lament, I may struggle to be with them in their joy. In all our intercessions, our experiences and relationship with the person we are praying for come into the prayer with us. Our view of them, frustrations with them, and understanding of their maturity influence how we pray. It is easy to focus, for instance, on the prodigal son's foolishness leading to his demise, when a famine is the stated reason why he was in need (Luke 15:14). We can do the same thing with brothers and sisters we think are foolish with their money, time, or health. When they ask for prayer, we might pray from our disapproval rather than from the grace and mercy of the Lord. This is where we need to consider Paul's calling for the people of God that "there may be no division in the body, but that the members may have the same care for one another. *If one member suffers, all suffer together; if one member is honored, all rejoice together*" (1 Cor. 12:25–26, emphasis added).

I find, at times, that I struggle to stay present in certain kinds of intercession. I think it is particularly difficult when, for one reason or another, I struggle to be empathetic to someone's circumstances. Sometimes other people's problems or life situations and scenarios seem foreign to my experience, so I struggle to enter into them. When this is the case, my mind wanders quickly to other things or I say a quick prayer for them and move on, never seeking to be present to them. Here, once again, I need to pause and intend to be with them—and with God—in their plight. But this requires that I give myself to a certain kind of watchfulness when I intercede and that my prayers are conditioned by how God has related to me. So, as I struggle to be present to them, I pray, "Lord, it was in my sins that you died for me. Help me be with them in their struggle, sin, and brokenness."

As we saw with the Lord's Prayer, it is easy to pray for someone in a way that isn't actually conditioned by forgiveness. A friend (or a spouse, parent, neighbor, etc.) who we are holding undigested angst against might ask for prayer, and we may dutifully pray for them without ever attending to what our heart is really doing. Maybe our prayer is conditioned by anxiety, where our anxiety alters how we pray for them and what we pray they will receive. Maybe we find ourselves unable to intercede in a way that is conditioned by "not my will, but yours, be done." Maybe our goal in intercession is to assert our will at all cost, and we pray to assure that God will get on board with *our* willing so the other person becomes who we want them to be.

When I was attacked online, it was easier to try *not* being present to that person and instead focus on my desire for justice. In seeking to be present to him in the Lord, however, my prayers were conditioned by "forgive as God has forgiven." As I stewed in my frustration and contemplated justice (or, more accurately, revenge), I didn't want to forgive. But before the Lord, holding someone whose life was no doubt filled with sadness, anxiety, and fear, I was able to be present to how those things have conditioned my own life with God. In being present to what was in my heart, I was able to move toward him in mercy.

In my own intercessions, I find that being present to God and to the person I am praying for takes intention and time. This is easier, however, than actually being present to myself. My heart will open wide in love for a friend suffering. I will hold them before the Father, seeking that his will be done on earth as it is in heaven in their lives, yet I am strangely absent. I want to be present to them. I want to be open to the ways my heart breaks for them (or doesn't) and the ways I avoid entering into their sorrow, fear, anxiety, or joy. I need to be open to the excuses I come up with for not being present to my experience in this. This is a training ground to be able to mourn with those who mourn and rejoice with those who rejoice (Rom. 12:15). It is a great gift to be able to enter into these realities and be truly present in them, sharing the victories, sorrows, and longings of those with whom we are united in Christ.

Present to God

The final form of presence in intercession is being present to God as we hold the other person and their request open before him. To be present to God in intercession calls our prayers into account with his love, particularly when they have become lazy or passionate attempts to pray *at* God rather than *to* him. To pray at God is to pray as if God were an object, as if he were some sort of vending machine we can push the right code into to get what we want. But

God has a will and a way that is not our way. When we intercede, we come to a God who is free and who loves us but does not owe us.

We need to be truly present to God, knowing by faith that he has set his face upon us. God isn't like the still-faced mother who has looked away from her child. When we take our negative events and feelings and project them back onto God, we often experience what feels like a still-faced father. In response, we start flailing in our seats and demanding our needs be met, hoping to get his attention, or we turn away with a lack of concern so we aren't let down again. But this pushes against the presence of God we know by faith. We must remember that God personally attends to us in Christ, already knows what we need, and cares for us as our Father. Our lives are hidden with Christ who is in God (Col. 3:3), and Christ is our great high priest who intercedes for us before the Father (Heb. 4:14; 7:25). All our prayers are caught up in the intercession of Christ to the Father who loves us. This frees us to be present to God without fear driving our prayers.

In our intercession, we should not try to lob prayers at God from a safe distance. In intercession, we place ourselves with others into God's loving gaze. As his children, we seek his will to be done in the lives of our brothers and sisters. We honestly bring our desires for them to our heavenly Father, holding them before his gaze, his love, and his mercy. Yet we must also be open to what is false in us or what we struggle to believe about his goodness because he feels hidden or far off. In intercession, we enter into joy, lament, or thanksgiving as we embrace our fellow believers in Christ. We pray that his will would be done in this circumstance, trusting that his will is always good even if we don't understand it.

To pray in God's presence is to actually be present to him in the full truth of who we have become, what we love, and how we struggle. In intercession, we draw near to the throne of grace in confidence *with another* and bring them with us to that throne, seeking his grace together. This means we should probably hesitate when we tell someone that we will pray for them. Too often I have told someone I would pray for them, thinking I might, but with no intention of really being present to God with this petition. If I did happen to remember, my prayer was usually a rushed, "Whoops, um, God help that person" kind of prayer. I hadn't counted the cost in telling someone I would be present to God with them in prayer.

In 1 Timothy 5:22, Paul warns Timothy not to be hasty in laying hands on another. In laying on of hands, just like with intercession, we are entering into the presence of God with each other; therefore, these are not matters to enter into lightly. If we do, we will make prayer a careless, nonrelational activity to relieve our guilt rather than entering into the presence of God to talk meaningfully. Intercession requires that we open our hearts to God and others, so we need to discern who we should open our hearts to and how to do so.

Open to Being Carried

One other reality of intercession can be overlooked. After wading through our own brokenness, the idea of focusing on others is a relief. Interceding seems like a way to pray well and feel good about praying well. But to truly embrace this vision of intercession, we must allow others to intercede for us. We cannot merely carry; we have to allow others to carry us. In the kingdom of God, no one person or group of people does all the heavy lifting. We are called to be one in love as the body of Christ (1 Cor. 12–13).

One of the difficulties in intercession is that we are so burdened by our own struggles that entering into someone else's can seem impossible. If that is the case, the solution is not to grit our teeth and do it but first to seek out the intercession of others. As brothers and sisters in Christ, we must partake in a kind of burden sharing that will allow us the space not merely to carry ourselves to the throne of grace but to carry others and be carried by them.

Therefore, the turn toward intercession for some is first to allow others to carry us before the Father in prayer. It is to trust others with the burdens of our souls rather than making light of them by focusing on other things. This does not mean we should share our burdens with everyone, but many find it difficult to share their struggles with anyone. It can feel safer, and maybe more "mature," to not allow others to pray for us. In this place, our self-talk can be something like, *I don't want to be a burden. It is not a big deal anyway. I don't want to bother them with these problems.* People who have no trouble sharing their burdens might need to begin by seeking out ways to carry others. Many of these folks need to intentionally commit to being present to someone else in prayer. For all of us, the Christian life is a continual giving and receiving of love where we are present with and present to each other in Christ by the Spirit.

As with all prayer, we are not alone in our efforts, nor do we create prayer or carry others in our own power. In our intercession, we are always carried along by the intercession of the Son and the Spirit. We embrace our intercessory calling from their acts of intercession. We bring others to God as we are carried along, with them, by the Son and the Spirit's faithfulness to be with us. When we don't know how to pray, and when we struggle to intercede, we trust in their intercessions, holding ourselves and others open to their prayers.

PRACTICE

Prayers of Petition and Intercession

Therefore, confess your sins to one another and pray for one another, that you may be healed. (James 5:16)

Bear one another's burdens, and so fulfill the law of Christ. (Gal. 6:2)

Unlike the other prayers we have considered in this book, intercession is not typically a set *kind* of prayer, as much as something you enter into as you pray. I find that when I am practicing a regular prayer of examine, particularly as I consider my day with the Lord, I have people brought to my attention for prayer. It is tempting, especially then, to have another agenda for my prayer time. I may want to focus on other parts of my day or turn to consider other things on my heart. But then I have to pause and enter into intercession. I must come to recognize this as an aspect of loving my neighbor as myself. Like all of our praying, there will be an intention and an act of recollection as we seek to be present to our brother or sister in Christ. Whatever my intention is, it must be conditioned by the Lord's Prayer.

It takes time to attend to the various ways we are called to be present in prayer. It takes practice to be able to focus on being with others, with ourselves, and with God as we pray. We must learn watchfulness to see how we are tempted not to be present in these ways, and it takes discernment to see how our own assumptions, impressions, and experiences guide our intercessions.

To enter into intercession more deeply, it will prove helpful to work through each of these three modes of presence:

1. *Intend to be present to the person and their situation.*
   Make room in your heart for this person and what they are experiencing. Take on their joy or their sorrow—and be present to it. Consider how you should pray for them and what would be a faithful way to pray as one present to them in the Spirit.

2. *Make sure you are present to yourself and your relationship with them.* If you are praying for someone close to you, you may already be caught up in their situation. Don't ignore how the situation affects you; instead, allow it to help you condition your prayers for them in the Spirit. With anyone we know well, we will need to be open to

ways we may feel frustrated with them, envious of them, or even annoyed that they asked us for prayer. Be open to this. The goal is not to shift away from the person you are praying for but to recognize the movement of your heart so you can pray for them and truly be present to them.

3. *Enter into what it means for you to be present to God with them.* You may not know what to pray for them, so hold them before the Lord. You may not know how to pull apart the messy emotions of your heart that are entwined in this circumstance, so bring it all to the Lord. Hold them in your heart as you pray the Lord's Prayer to further condition your prayer. As you do, pause for a moment when you pray "our" Father. Bring them with you as you pray with God, bound up in the life of Christ by the power of his Spirit who binds all things together in love.

If you would like something more structured, you can try several things.

Share with the Lord, in the most unvarnished way, exactly what you want and what you would like to see happen on behalf of another person. Draw near with boldness to the Father to find mercy, grace, and help in a time of need. At this point, do not censor your prayer. Come as you are, and come as you really feel and think about this matter. Your Father cares, so come.

Reality-test your prayer. Ask the Lord to search your heart with that prayer (in Ps. 139:23–24 fashion) to see what was really driving it. See if some pain, worry, anxiety, frustration, anger, or other matter was motivating the prayer for them. Don't fix or hide anything. Just share with God and open your heart to him. Learn from him who cares and accepts you, and come to him whose yoke is easy and whose burden is light (Matt. 11:28–30).

Open your heart to the person you are praying for. Consider whether your heart is loving or open to that person, or if it is closed or not caring toward them. Tell God what you discover. Ask God to open your heart to this person as Paul encouraged the Corinthians (2 Cor. 6:11). Is this easy or are there impediments?

Remind yourself of your request in light of the truth that God already knows what you need before you ask. Consider whether you really believe that—and ask for God to help your unbelief. Remind yourself that he is your Father, and he cares for you and the person you are praying for. Bring this all to the Lord and tell him your reaction—truth, confusion, doubt, worry, or whatever else may be accurate for you. Ask him to have mercy and help you, even in your prayers, and to have mercy for the person you are praying for.

Turn again to interceding for the other person. Take your request, with all the possible tensions, and bring it to God again. Ask for mercy and grace for yourself and the person you are praying for. Rest in the truth that you do not know how to pray, but the Spirit is always praying for you according to the will of God (Rom. 8:26). Trust that as you intercede, you do so within the intercession of the Son and the Spirit, and share in their work.

CONCLUSION

The Struggle and Joy of Petition

If then you have been raised with Christ, seek the things that are above,
where Christ is, seated at the right hand of God. Set your minds on
things that are above, not on things that are on earth. For you have
died, and your life is hidden with Christ in God. When Christ who is
your life appears, then you also will appear with him in glory. . . . Put
on then, as God's chosen ones, holy and beloved, compassionate hearts,
kindness, humility, meekness, and patience, bearing with one another
and, if one has a complaint against another, forgiving each other; as
the Lord has forgiven you, so you also must forgive. And above all these
put on love, which binds everything together in perfect harmony. And
let the peace of Christ rule in your hearts, to which indeed you were
called in one body. And be thankful. Let the word of Christ dwell in you
richly, teaching and admonishing one another in all wisdom, singing
psalms and hymns and spiritual songs, with thankfulness in your hearts
to God. And whatever you do, in word or deed, do everything in the
name of the Lord Jesus, giving thanks to God the Father through him.

Colossians 3:1–4, 12–17

If you consider the passages above, you discover the vision of
prayer we've outlined in this book. Our lives are hidden with
Christ in God, with the One who prays for us and from within us,

so that we, too, can boldly ascend to the throne of grace. These truths used to seem too high for us. Yet as we came out of hiding to share our souls with the Lord, we discovered he really is there with us—loving us and praying for us. It became clear that prayer becomes real when we are truly present to the Lord. In the presence of God, we discover our hearts are "naked and exposed" to him (Heb. 4:13). God sees all and knows all, so we come in the truth of what he sees and knows.

As children of our Father in heaven, we seek to "put on" the life of Christ. Prayer is the training ground to really know this is true and to live as if it were true. In this training, we learn to bear with one another and lift each other up to the Lord. In this training, the Lord binds our hearts together in the harmony of his love (Col. 3:14). In "putting on" Christ, we seek to love the Lord with our whole heart and our neighbor as ourselves. This does not happen by accident but requires that we enter into the prayers of others (the Lord's Prayer and the Psalms). In conditioning our prayers through Scripture, we seek a new intention to be with God in all things, recollecting our hearts to him and examining our lives in his presence. These help form us in his presence and for his presence, so that we, too, can be united in love with others in the Spirit of God, interceding for and blessing one another.

A Struggle of Love

The problem we face is that prayer is much easier to read or write about than to practice. It is easy to understand that we should be honest in prayer. The refrain "You can say anything to God" has become cliché. Entering into that honesty is an entirely different reality. Seeing how your previous experiences and relationships have formed your expectations is easier said than done. It is difficult to see how many assumptions we bring into prayer with us. Perhaps most difficult is seeing that prayer is a struggle when we didn't anticipate it would be. The struggle of prayer, however, is not for its own sake but for the sake of deeper love, communion, and trust in the Lord who is present to you, even to the depths of your soul.

Prayer is a struggle, but it is a struggle of love. Our difficulties in prayer are like the struggles of friendship, parenting, and marriage. These are struggles to be with another in truth, even when the truth is difficult. Just as with marriage and friendship, it requires vulnerability to open our hearts and seek help. It can be difficult to share our desires and name the things we long for.

As a struggle of love, prayer should also be a journey into joy. This might not seem obvious. Seeing the truth of ourselves in the presence of God and learning new modes of praying that help to break open one's heart before the Lord may not seem to instill joy. The truth of our lives before God may seem heavy, and while honesty may seem necessary, many wonder if it will be joyful. While prayer does involve struggle, it is through this struggle that we find freedom. To be seen and known in the love, grace, mercy, and forgiveness of God is where our hearts come alive. To be with God—really with him in the truth of our lives—is where we discover the joy of prayer.

Petitioning God

At its most basic level, prayer is petitioning God. In petitioning God, we ask him whatever is on our hearts. This is like the prayer of a child, who isn't tempted to pray for the "right" things but who prays her every desire. We, too, need to rediscover the prayer of simple faith. Nothing is simpler than to come to God with our urgent needs and requests, yet few things press us into deep places in our hearts. So we pray,

"Oh, God, don't let my mother die."
"Oh, God, save me from my sin."
"Oh, God, heal my child."

"Oh, God, help my failing business."

"Oh, God, I just don't know what to do; help me!"

What starts off as simple, with time and age becomes more complex. I remember going to a prayer meeting for a friend with cancer. Entire families from church showed up to cry out to God on behalf of him and his family. We stood in his driveway because his compromised immune system wouldn't allow us to see him face-to-face, and we prayed. As we went around praying, most of us prayed as adults tend to. We asked God for wisdom for the doctors. We thanked God for his provisions over our friend and his family. We thanked God for our friend. Then the group paused for a moment, and the silence was broken by a smaller voice. A child simply prayed, "God, don't let him die."

No one had yet used the words *death* or *die*. But when that child prayed, you could feel the whole group sigh an "amen." That child prayed what we all wanted to pray. That child spoke the truth of our hearts. As adults, we tend not to lay out our prayers, at least not publicly, as boldly as that child did. We hedge and consider what the right way to pray might be. That child's prayer, however, cut through all of this to speak the truth of our hearts.

As we mature, sometimes our growth in knowledge is not what we had hoped it would be. We assume that growing in knowledge will mean having fewer questions, but it often works the other way around. Our development often raises new and more complicated questions. We stop praying like that child because when we do, in all of that vulnerability, we remember times when God didn't seem to hear. What our experiences teach us about God, ourselves, and our petitions proves messier than we expected. As we mature, we do increase in knowledge. We know God doesn't need to be cajoled or manipulated by our requests, that he already knows what we need (Matt. 6:7–8). In our maturity, we know God has a will—and we know it may differ from ours. But we also know we pray for things we think God *should* will and for things we know he does will—and still wait for our prayers to be answered.

The Christian journey includes growing in knowledge, but growth in knowledge does not necessarily make the Christian life easier, nor does it clear up all the struggles we might have. We cannot merely affirm that God is God and God will do what he wants. That might seem like a faithful response, but it isn't how the psalmists prayed, and it isn't how Jesus prayed. We have to struggle with God in prayer. We have to struggle with the reality that he is God and does what he wants, yet the world doesn't seem to look like that. We have to struggle when our most heartfelt prayers are not answered as we desire. Christian prayer is never a solution to our struggle with God's ways being different from our own; it is how we bring our will to him. We must not bypass the struggle, because sometimes the Lord calls us into it to know who he is truly, to know who we are, and to lay ourselves down at his feet. As our unanswered prayers move us from frustration to questioning if God cares about our circumstances at all, the struggle of faith is to keep praying, "Lord, I believe, but help me here in my unbelief." But some of us have allowed the struggle to lead us into prayer-lessness. Sometimes we stop praying because we wonder whether our prayers make any difference. The following questions emerge:

"Do I even care about what I am praying for?"
"Does God even hear or care, or does he only hear his will?"
"Is he too busy, or is this not important enough to him?"
"Have I not done enough for him? Should I pray harder and with more faith?"
"Do I care enough to pray harder?"

In these times, simple petitions raise some of the deepest, darkest beliefs we have about God, ourselves, and others.

Maturing in prayer and our life with God will lead us into two key realities that are easier to memorize than to really internalize in our hearts. First, God has a will. Second, God's ways are not our ways (Isa. 55:8).

When we petition God, we are presenting our hearts to him. Maybe we can't even articulate our desires. We just feel them and offer them to him. As we do so, knowing he has a will, we pray the prayer of Jesus, "Not my will, but yours, be done" (Luke 22:42). God's ways are not our ways, and God's will isn't always what I will. We do not understand why God responds or chooses not to, and even this needs to be conditioned by that prayer of Jesus—again, "Lord, not my will, but yours, be done." Like Paul, who pleaded with the Lord to take the thorn from his flesh, we have to be open to hearing that the Lord is leading us to the desert or disciplining us for our good. Like Paul, we still name our desires (2 Cor. 12:8). Like Jesus, we still ask what is on our hearts (Luke 22:42).

The struggle to lay down our will to embrace God's will is the struggle to pray like Jesus. What we mustn't do is simply affirm God's will to stop the struggle from beginning in the first place. It is too easy to say, "God is God, and he will do what he wants" without actually engaging him deeply about what this does in our hearts. When Paul was given a thorn in the flesh, it led him to the Lord to struggle. When Christ was called to the cross, it led him to the Father to struggle. What is your invitation to struggle with the Lord in this season of life? How are you accepting or rejecting the call to be with him in these places and not asserting truths that, however true, may shut down your struggling or lead you away from being honest?

We come as a child to our Father, but we come trusting that he has a will and his ways are not our ways. When a child requests something from her parents, she is usually open only to her request. As we mature, we must come to hold our requests open to God's will and whether we care about God's will at all. We seek to ponder what is really going on inside ourselves when we offer petitions to God. The child isn't terribly concerned with the will of the parents, unless, of course, the parents' will is contrary to her will, and then she seeks to manipulate it to match her own. In maturity, we are led down a different path, however much we still find ourselves secretly trying to manipulate God in prayer. In maturity, we must be open to God in our petitions, especially ones we know are good but do not care much about. We need to be open to God when praying for something that grabs us at the core of our being, when we secretly worry God may disagree with what we deeply desire.

We will doubt and grow weary in our petitions. We will, at times, wonder what the use of praying is at all. So we tell him exactly that. We lament in the presence of God, who gazes upon us in love. We come as those who are in Christ, knowing that as Jesus intercedes for us, we are called to draw near with confidence to find mercy and grace. We come as those who don't know how to pray as we ought (Rom. 8:26); therefore, we pray, "Oh, Lord, you know. You see all. Lord, have mercy."

This is why prayer can never simply be a topic to understand or a technique to master. Prayer is being with God in truth and love. Because of this, there are several emphases in prayer that we reflect on in conclusion. These emphases are mini callings for prayer—invitations to a deep life of prayer. Above all, these are invitations into love.

Intend to Be with God as He Really Is

When we remember God descending with fire on Mount Sinai and calling us to fear him, we are recollected around the truths that God's ways are not our ways, that he is God and we are not, and that no thought, idea, building, or power could somehow contain him. Yet as his children, we know this is good news.

When we remember that the fear of the Lord is the beginning of wisdom, we must also recall that perfect love casts out fear (Prov. 9:10; 1 John 4:18). We need to name our fears, and we need to seek the One who is perfect love. Our fear should turn us toward him to set our minds on him and trust that he is our hope. In our brokenness and sin, we seek help elsewhere, but we have no hope outside of Christ. We must continually come to him and seek him as the One who casts out fear.

We are often tempted, instead, to make God less (less judging, less sovereign, less powerful) than he is. This is a failure to truly embrace God as God. To know God as merciful is not to make him less judging but to affirm the truth of the cross. We were dead in our trespasses before the Lord whom we are to fear, yet God has made us alive together with Christ, "having forgiven us all our trespasses, by canceling the record of debt that stood against us with its legal demands. This he set aside, nailing it to the cross" (Col. 2:13–14). The cross shows that God didn't decide to take sin less seriously. God didn't decide that his justice and judgment were minor realities he could ignore. God simultaneously raised the stakes as high as they could go and on the cross showed himself to be merciful, kind, and gracious to us.

Intend to Be with God in Reality, and Resist Turning to Fantasy and Prayers of Magic

Second, we need to intend to be with God *in reality*. The problem with our fantasy lives before God is that fantasy can often feel like what God is calling us to. In our deepest places, we fear that God does not want us as we really are, so instead of drawing near to him, we send our Christian avatar to pray. Our avatar looks the part of the good Christian but is not who we truly are. In doing so, we falsely assume God wants us to mine our own internal resources to fix our lives and grow ourselves, *and only then come to him*. But this is self-help, a kind of fantasy, and not the life of grace. Fantasy, however, is deceptive, and we can fail to see it clearly. Fantasy is anything we turn to outside of Christ to ground our value, our identity, and our goodness. Fantasy is our fleshly strategy not to live in the truth. Our call is always against fantasy to embrace reality. This means we must name the truth of where our heart does go, or wants to go, outside of Christ and then intend to be with him in those places.

Intend to Be Honest with God in All the Longings of Your Heart, and Resist Cleaning Them Up to Appear More Acceptable

Third, because we are called into reality rather than fantasy, we must resist the temptation to clean ourselves up. Instead, we need to foster a relationship with God that trades in honesty. Honesty is the great virtue of Christian prayer, which is why true Christian praying should always bear the fruit of humility. Our journey of prayer starts by naming the truth and offering ourselves to God. In doing so, we take on the prayer, "I believe, help me in my unbelief." We pray, "Lord, I don't want to clean myself up before you. I don't want to clothe myself in your presence. I want to embrace Christ's robes of righteousness. Father, I am already clean in Christ because of the word he has spoken to me [John 15:3], so let this word dwell in me richly [Col. 3:16]." This is not yet true of every aspect of our hearts. As we abide in the Lord in truth, he will lead us to the place where we can say these words from the deepest places of our souls.

Intend to Live in the Truth of Who You Are in Christ, and Resist Grounding Yourself in Self-Constructed Identities

Last, the person who prays in faith is the one seeking to be recollected to who they are in Christ. This is our calling to lay down the old man (Adam) and embrace the new man (Christ) as our identity. We are no longer defined from within by what we do and what we achieve but by whose we are. We are God's. We are his children. He is our Father. This is the defining reality for our prayers, and not what our hearts do in God's presence. Our experience in prayer does not define us, nor does it tell us if prayer is "going well." We are called to God by faith, trusting in who he is, trusting that he meets us in reality, and trusting that we don't need to clean ourselves up before coming to him. Come to your heavenly Father in Christ by grace, and trust that Christ is victorious for you.

As you consider your prayer life, how might these emphases help you reorient what you have been doing (or not doing) and discern what you should be giving yourself to? This is the concluding question of this book. What forms of prayer should you take on? This is not a question you should answer quickly, but one you should wrestle with. You need to discern what you should give yourself to.

That said, we do believe all these prayers, or something like them, should be a foundational and regular part of a Christian's prayer life. They won't all be part of a daily routine. They don't have to look identical to how we describe them in this book. But praying the Psalms, intending to present yourself to God, recollecting your heart to him, examining your life, and interceding for others should all form a life of deep prayer. The Lord's Prayer, likewise, should condition and shape all Christian praying. Toward that end, we have included the "Practicing" sections for each chapter in the Table of Contents so you can flip back there easily. We have also included several appendices at the back that will help you enter into these prayers more deeply. These structures are helpful scaffolding as you rediscover what prayer can be. We hope these tools will be meaningful as you seek out a deeper life of prayer.

We grow in prayer only by praying, even though prayer alone doesn't guarantee that we grow in depth. Recall the Pharisee at the temple who prayed, "God, I thank you that I am not like other men, extortioners, unjust, adulterers, or even like this tax collector. I fast twice a week; I give tithes of all that I get" (Luke 18:11–12). Prayer did not lead to growth for him because he failed to realize who God truly is and, therefore, who he was before the Lord. Instead, it was the person who prayed in truth who grew in depth. It was not the morally upright Pharisee, but the tax collector, who threw himself on the mercy of the Lord, praying, "Be merciful to me, a sinner!" who Jesus tells us left that place justified. Prayer, by itself, can be used to further engrain our fleshliness, which is why we must seek the truth.

To grow in prayer requires that one is open to God as he really is—and open to the truth of oneself in his presence. This means we have to be watchful in prayer, as Scripture instructs us, and open to what our longings, desires, and experiences in prayer reveal about our hearts. What we find in our hearts provides the fodder for prayer and leads us down the path to know God deeply. In our honesty we trust that he is the One who hears all because he sees all, and we embrace the truth that he is already doing the deep praying in our souls. Our prayer rests on the action of God to redeem, reconcile, and unite us to himself. May our prayers be a continual exclamation that God has done all so that we can pray all.

GROUP LEADER'S GUIDE

Overview

Before turning to specifics, we suggest that the following components are necessary for groups going through the book:

- A time to discuss the chapter that group members have read for that meeting and address any questions, worries, or insights
- A time for each person to share about what the prayer exercise was like for them
- Finally, a time to pray together, holding open before the Lord what each member is learning, what prayer has been like for them, and what they believe the Lord may be calling them into

After we expand on each of these sections below, we raise further issues to ponder as you think about leading this group well. Our hope is that these groups can be a place to practice and learn deep prayer together.

Group Logistics

Since every chapter of the book includes a practice, we think it is important that each person read the chapter and spend some time practicing the prayer exercise before meeting. The praying is where all the action takes place. It is one thing to talk about prayer and not pray; it is a whole other thing to pray and then talk about prayer. Prayer reveals our hearts and leads us to face ourselves honestly in ways few other practices do.

If you meet weekly, then sometime during the week each person should read the chapter and do the prayer exercise at the end. It may prove helpful for everyone to have a journal to write down thoughts, questions, and reflections on their time, focusing on what it was like, how they went about practicing the prayer, and how they feel about the time they spent with the Lord. Was it frustrating? Did they spend the whole time trying to wrestle a wandering mind? Did they fall asleep? Did they wonder where God was? Was it insightful or boring? However people choose to reflect on these things, they should come to the group time having read the chapter, done the prayer exercise, and reflected on the time.

The following elements should comprise each meeting. First, take time for each participant to share what their prayer time was like, what really took place, and what insights, experiences, questions, or confusions emerged. The book calls for honest, unvarnished prayer, so now is the time to encourage people to share honestly with one another about their experience. It is important to be heard and to hear others. It may confirm, convict, or affirm what is going on in one's relationship with the Lord. Importantly, you should not try to "rescue" members, suggesting quick and easy fixes. Rather, your goal is to encourage each participant to see how God is working in all things (whether we consider them negative or positive). God is always working and calling us into love. It will be especially important for you, as the leader, to model this—not trying to fix the group members or help them hide but guiding them to see how God is always working and loving us in our lives (and maybe especially in our failures).

Second, as you begin to share with and listen to one another, you can also spend time addressing any questions or conundrums that arose from the readings or the prayer experience. Do not assume everyone should just accept at face value what has been written here. It is important for people to wrestle with the thoughts and suggestions on prayer in this book, to test ideas, and to search Scripture to determine the truth, falsities, or half-truths. Don't push this off. God gave us minds to guard the gates of our hearts against falsehood and to permit the truth to come in. Of course, sometimes we are deceived and can be dishonest with ourselves about ideas and push them off too hastily. But be patient with one another as you explore these issues. You should help this process and shepherd honest dialogue about the book.

Third, pray together. Instead of asking for prayer requests, we suggest you bring your thoughts, feelings, and experiences in reading the book and practicing the prayer exercise to the Lord through prayer itself. You, as the leader, will set the tone for the group by modeling what it looks like to bring these things into prayer. Also invite each member to hold one another before the Lord and encourage them to pray about things they are learning, questions they might have, and their experience in the prayer exercise. To the degree each of them are willing and trust the group, ask them to open their lives to the Lord and to one another. Have them lift up to him any worries, anxieties, and fears. After you go around the group, close in prayer, bringing all these things before the Lord and holding the group open to his intercession.

This is exactly how John and I, along with the other members of our executive team, begin our regular meetings. Every other week during the semester, we come together, meditate through John 15, and open our hearts to the Lord and to one another. Sometimes we hear of trials we were not aware of. Other times we hear of concerns we did not know were burdening anyone other than ourselves. Sometimes we get to rejoice together, and at other times we lament. But every time, we bring our lives to the Lord, opening to him and to one another and seeking his will in all things. This is the vision of these groups—that you would learn to pray with and for one another and that you would learn to open wide your hearts to the Lord.

This kind of group is easy to explain but probably more difficult for folks to embrace. It will take a bit of time, we imagine, for folks to really enter into this kind of prayer with one another (unless the group already has depth in vulnerability). To foster this, we have included some further questions that may be helpful to consider. The remainder of this leader's guide attends to two questions that will be important for you to think through before the group begins. First, it is important to ponder and dialogue about group expectations. The expectations you have as the group leader, and the expectations of each participant, will shape what the group is and how people relate in it. Second, we want you to consider the various difficulties with group prayer. The former is straightforward, the latter is more pressing.

Setting Up the Group

It may prove helpful to meet before you begin the book to ask what each participant hopes to gain from this study. As you're the leader of this group, the first question you have to ask is about your own hopes and expectations, and then ask about the hopes and expectations of others. What do we hope will come of this? Some expectations won't be met. Some expectations will be unrealistic. But what *should* our expectations be? We may not ponder this often, but it is important to do so. If you could narrow down your hopes to one thing, what would it be? Do you hope you will "figure out" prayer so that it will finally make sense? Do you hope you will be able to know all the right things about prayer? As you verbalize your hopes for the group and hear the thoughts of others, take time to reality-test the feasibility of these expectations. Address how the goals of this book may or may not align with group expectations.

If you raise the question for the whole group, it is important to point out any conflicting expectations. Furthermore, it will be helpful to simply ask: "What do the expectations, desires, and hopes we bring into this group have to do with prayer? What expectations do we have, if any, about growing together in prayer?" Our hopes and expectations often end up defining how we judge whether a small group experience is "good" or "bad." If someone comes hoping to solely learn new information, they will be annoyed if there is a lot of time for conversation and community. They do not want community and that isn't their expectation, so they will judge a group that focuses on community to be bad or else just a waste of *their* time. Others will have the exact opposite sense. They are desperate for community and may not care about gaining any new information. They just want devoted time to share life with others.

Whatever expectations you and your group bring to this time, you have freedom to craft the group to address them. If people want community, then community should be a key component. If people want to wrestle through aspects of the book, then a lengthier time of open discussion should be a regular part of your rhythm (however often you decide the group should meet). But what we see as a nonnegotiable to this group study is discussion and prayer. Because this is a book on prayer, it won't ultimately be helpful to simply answer questions and discuss the content of the book. For certain topics this might be more helpful, but not for prayer. We want you to move beyond discussing ideas about praying to actually praying.

The Difficulties of Group Prayer

This book encourages honest, unvarnished prayers with the Lord, learning to pray in secret to our Father who hears and repays in secret (Matt. 6:6). The prayer exercises for each chapter might lead you into wonderful times, but maybe also some raw, heated, unnerving, lamenting, angry, depressed times. You may find yourself saying things to the Lord that you really do not want anyone else to hear or even know.

While our prayer to the Father in secret should be unvarnished, our time together should not be (at least not in the same manner). When you come to pray together, you should not expect that each of you will pray in the same manner as you did alone. This is the tension we will face in our groups. We want to learn to pray honestly and meaningfully together. But some things only God should hear (and perhaps can hear). Unvarnished prayer is necessary between you and the Lord; if it is in your heart, it must be shared. Nothing in your heart, no matter how raw and unclean, is for you alone. The Lord becomes our teacher and lover to help us metabolize these elements and find him in all things. Though you may find another person to help you process this, such as a pastor or Christian counselor, most groups we are part of do not play this role.

The kind of groups we are discussing are for meaningful sharing about prayer and meaningful praying. I want to distinguish between *unvarnished* and *meaningful*. Some things are so raw that they will not encourage others and might even confuse them. That is, we want you to learn how to navigate with the Lord what is raw in your heart and what can be meaningful for dialogue and prayer with others. *Group prayer is not the same as personal prayer.* Group prayer may still come out as raw, but the deepest place in the soul is, in some ways, only for God.

The tension is to be honest with integrity, not unreal or shiny, but in such a way that edifies as well. The temptation to go back to our repressed, almost dishonest prayers with others is always there. The opposite is a temptation as well, when we fail to distinguish between our unvarnished prayer with the Lord and our prayers with others. It may be important, as a leader, to raise these issues with the group, and to make one of the goals of the group an ongoing discussion to discern how to properly pray "publicly" together. It may feel forced, or messy, or awkward at times, but it is helpful to talk about this as well. Just keep in mind: group prayer is not the same as private prayer.

As a leader, you will have to explain the tension folks will feel between their private and public prayers—though most will feel this tension already—and how to enter into it. Encourage each person to share as they feel comfortable and foster a group that is safe, encouraging, and open. Much of what you will do as a leader is model this. One of the key elements to this is that we are not interested in participants trying to fix one another or their prayer lives but rather to look for ways to point one another to Christ. The goal is not to correct what others share but to point to Christ. Coming to Christ is the goal.

As the group leader, your role is not to model perfection or to prove you are "further along" than others in the group. Your role is to model vulnerability, wisdom, and integrity. That is often the hardest role of a leader, but it is not your only one. You will also need to model how people respond to the truth. They will often want to judge their experience in prayer: "I had a bad prayer time" or "I was really off in prayer." We tend to think that what God wants for us is to know we are bad and to try harder. That isn't, however, what we are calling you to do in this book. We need to name the truth of our prayer life, precisely because prayer is not a place to be good but a place to be honest. That is true in community as well. At times this will mean reminding folks that the goal is honesty in prayer, because we have to remember that God knows we don't know how to pray as we ought, which is why he prays for us. His prayers are perfect, his prayers are enough, and yet his prayers call us to pray. Our encouragement is to prod one another to offer ourselves in truth to the God who knows all and sees all.

APPENDIX 1

A Guide for Personally Praying the Psalms

Below are examples of psalms and how we have prayed these in our own lives (we have made them a bit more generic for your use). You will see the psalm and underneath find our own expansion in our prayers in italics. These are examples for you to consider as you begin to pray.

Psalm 3: A Lament and Petition

The superscription tells us that it is a Psalm of David when he fled from his son Absalom (during the rebellion). Absalom is not mentioned in the psalm itself; therefore, we are invited to wrestle with any adversaries we have. You, the pray-er, are invited to read your life into this. The key is to *pray the psalm*, throw yourself into the psalm, open yourself to the Lord, and see what happens. If possible, we encourage you pray it out loud.

> **Superscription:** A Psalm of David, when he fled from Absalom, his son.

> *Lord, I recall Absalom—betrayed his very own dad, yet his dad was messed up too! What a mess.*

O LORD, how many are my foes! (v. 1)

David and Absalom, yes, they had their problems! But God, I, too, have my foes, enemies, and struggles. I have internal foes that seem endless.

Many are rising against me; (v. 1)

God, there are so many hassles in my life. Lord, there are so many struggles.

many are saying of my soul,
"There is no salvation for him in God." (v. 2)

Yes, Lord, will you help? The world and the devil say you are not there, that you won't help. O God, am I alone in this?

But you, O LORD, are a shield about me,
my glory, and the lifter of my head. (v. 3)

God, I believe this—that you are a shield. But I wish to believe this more. Help my unbelief! Be with me in my problems, O Lord. Be a shield. I know you have been a shield. Lord, I come to you.

I cried aloud to the LORD,
and he answered me from his holy hill. (v. 4)

O God! You have answered me before, you have delivered me from my problems and struggles and adversaries. O Lord, deliver me and answer me! Lord, I cry to you, please help!

I lay down and slept;
I woke again, for the LORD sustained me. (v. 5)

Lord, I cannot handle these things in my life—sleep is the only rest from them. O Lord, thank you that when I wake, you are there. It is so good to know rest. Lord, you know that sometimes I can't sleep, so open my heart to you—to trust. Look at how I open my heart to myself in bed as if you are not here. Lord, help me pour it out to you. Lord, be with me.

> I will not be afraid of many thousands of people
> who have set themselves against me all around. (v. 6)

Lord, this is my commitment as long as you are near me. O God, strengthen my heart to trust you! Lord, at times I have felt alone. O God, be with me—give me courage to endure the struggles and trials.

> Arise, O LORD!
> Save me, O my God! (v. 7)

This is my prayer, this is why I came to you—O God, arise, step up. Why don't you rescue me and deliver me from all of this? Lord, please answer me and save me in this situation.

> For you strike all my enemies on the cheek;
> you break the teeth of the wicked. (v. 7)

You say you will—will you—one day, now? God, judge the wicked, the demonic, the enemies of you and me. Lord, answer me in my struggles. O Lord, have mercy. God, help.

> Salvation belongs to the LORD;
> your blessing be on your people! (v. 8)

God, in you alone there is deliverance—not in my cleverness. Hear my cries for deliverance, for help. Help me trust and believe that there is full salvation and blessing in you alone. O God, bless us, bless us, be with us! Hear my prayers. Amen. Amen. Amen.

Psalm 117: A Praise Psalm

> Praise the LORD, all nations!
> Extol him, all peoples! (v. 1)

Lord, I do praise you! Lord, even when my heart says I do not care, even when my heart is heavy, you are still worthy of praise. It is still good to praise you. And now, I do praise you. But Lord, those times when my heart is in the dust, I will tell you the truth of where my heart is—and yet you are still worthy of praise. Lord, please have mercy on me when my heart fails to praise you, when I am under the wave. O Lord, have mercy. Praise you.

> For great is his steadfast love toward us, (v. 2)

Yes, Lord, you never fail us. Great is your lovingkindness— your covenant loyalty toward us. Thank you so much. Praise you! Thank you that you are so faithful to us in Christ. Bless you, O Jesus. Bless you, Father. Bless you, Spirit. When I faint in my thanks and praise, your steadfast love is ever with me. Bless you.

> and the faithfulness of the LORD endures forever. (v. 2)

Praise you for your faithfulness, O Lord. Thank you so much that you are faithful when I am so faithless. It is your constancy— not my own—that gives me hope. So much so that when I am in despair, I will still praise you for your faithfulness. And even when I fail, you never fail me.

> Praise the LORD! (v. 2)

Amen and Amen.

Psalm 139: A Lament—and Prayer of Imprecation and Petition*

O LORD, You have searched me and known me. (v. 1)

God, you know everything about me—I am like transparent glass to you.

> You know when I sit down and when I rise up;
> You understand my thought from afar. (v. 2)

You are always with me—there is no space from you. You are with me always. You understand all my thoughts, better than even I do.

> You scrutinize my path and my lying down, (v. 3)

You, O God, have X-ray vision into me—always looking, evaluating, seeing what I don't even see. There is no ambiguity with you. O God, have mercy. Lord, I am so glad there is mercy for us in Christ! You see all and know all, but you see me in a gaze of love. O Lord, if this were not so, who could stand?

> And are intimately acquainted with all my ways. (v. 3)

You know all my motives; you live right inside of me. Nothing is hidden from you.

> Even before there is a word on my tongue,
> Behold, O Lord, You know it all. (v. 4)

You can predict all I am going to say—I am so predictable to you. You know me so well.

*All verses from Psalm 139 are NASB.

You have enclosed me behind and before, (v. 5)

There is no turning from your sight. You have trapped me in. Your sight is good, Lord, but it can feel like I'm surrounded and undone.

And laid Your hand upon me. (v. 5)

Lord, is this good or bad that I feel hemmed in? God, you know all my thoughts and ways. There is no escaping your knowing me, that you are also with me. O Lord, you know all. I am yours.

Such knowledge is too wonderful for me;
It is too high, I cannot attain to it. (v. 6)

Is it too much to be so transparent before you, God? I feel undone before you. Sometimes it is such a comfort to be here, Lord, and sometimes it is confusing. Blessed Lord, be merciful to me.

Where can I go from Your Spirit?
Or where can I flee from Your presence? (v. 7)

Yes, Lord, how can I get space from you? I cannot—again, this is sometimes so wonderful to me. But sometimes, Lord, I want a moment by myself—I don't always want to be seen! In one sense, it is good. But, Lord, as I come back to my senses, what would happen if I was left alone? Bless you, Lord, bless you.

If I ascend to heaven, You are there;
If I make my bed in Sheol, behold, You are there. (v. 8)

Lord, in heaven or in death, you are there—even in the darkest place of death and disaster and pain, you are there. God, I cannot even be in the pits by myself.

> If I take the wings of the dawn,
> If I dwell in the remotest part of the sea, (v. 9)

Even if I want to get away, I cannot—God, that is so good. And also, there is no privacy with you! Can I handle this?

> Even there Your hand will lead me,
> And Your right hand will lay hold of me. (v. 10)

Lord, bless you for this—that even in the pits, you will lead and be with me. O God, sometimes I have not felt this—be with me. Help me believe your love is with me.

> If I say, "Surely the darkness will overwhelm me,
> And the light around me will be night,"
> Even the darkness is not dark to You,
> And the night is as bright as the day.
> Darkness and light are alike to You. (vv. 11–12)

O God, it doesn't matter. Either way, you see all, and you are with all of me. When I am afraid and confused, you know what is going on in my life. It is all light to you. Help me to trust you in this.

> For You formed my inward parts;
> You wove me in my mother's womb. (v. 13)

Lord, this goes even deeper—you made me in such a way that all is known to you! God, my whole life is in your hands, completely known by you.

> I will give thanks to You, for I am fearfully and
>   wonderfully made;
> Wonderful are Your works,
> And my soul knows it very well. (v. 14)

It is amazing! And God, when my soul is not amazed by this truth, it is still amazing. Help my soul to know this well in Jesus.

> My frame was not hidden from You,
> When I was made in secret,
> And skillfully wrought in the depths of the earth;
> Your eyes have seen my unformed substance;
> And in Your book were all written
> The days that were ordained for me,
> When as yet there was not one of them. (vv. 15–16)

God, you know it all! My entire life is before you, and nothing is hidden.

> How precious also are Your thoughts to me, O God!
> How vast is the sum of them! (v. 17)

It really is amazing, God, how much you think of me. Nothing escapes you!

> If I should count them, they would outnumber the sand.
> When I awake, I am still with You. (v. 18)

I go to a place I don't even know in my dreams, and then you are there when I awake. Lord, you know me better than I do! I even get tired of me, and I go to sleep! But you never tire of knowing me. O Lord, open my heart to this truth, for sometimes I am so dull to hear and believe that you are with me, that you even want to know and be with me.

Notice: And now comes the petition that the psalmist wanted to ask: "God, because you know me so well and nothing is hidden from you—I might as well tell you exactly what is in my heart . . ."

> O that You would slay the wicked, O God;
> Depart from me, therefore, men of bloodshed. (v. 19)

Lord, there are people who are after me, who are my adversar-ies, who so bother me and are evil. I want them all dead. I want them gone, out of my life! God, just kill them! Take them away! Take this trial away!

> For they speak against You wickedly, (v. 20)

God, they are your enemies too, not just mine!

> And Your enemies take Your name in vain. (v. 20)

They are evil. They don't believe in you; they don't love you.

> Do I not hate those who hate You, O LORD?
> And do I not loathe those who rise up against You?
> I hate them with the utmost hatred;
> They have become my enemies. (vv. 21–22)

They hate you, and I hate them—kill them! Lord, deal with them. I am so tired of them and what they are doing in my life, in my culture, and in others' lives. O Lord, help, save, deliver, and defend us, O God, by your grace.

Notice: This is a turning point in the prayer in which he turns out of anger to God in prayer, and now his heart is open to let God teach him in the sanctuary of prayer. Just maybe God will change your heart as you speak honestly.

> Search me, O God, and know my heart;
> Try me and know my anxious thoughts; (v. 23)

Lord, I just asked you to kill these people who hate me, who I hate, who are violent, who are wicked and so bothersome. O Lord, O Lord, search me and test what is in my heart—should I pray that way? God, they are evil. Surely you will judge them someday—why not now? They have no interest in you at all or in doing good! And maybe they are even believers, but I want them out of my life! O God, search my heart.

> And see if there be any hurtful [literally "painful"] way in
> me, (v. 24)

God, is this just my own revenge? Just because I have anger and it seems like a righteous cause does not mean my heart is clean. Maybe I hate them because they have hurt me and are a bother to me, my life, and my culture. O God, what is my pain in this? What is theirs? Lord, open my heart to the truth.

> And lead me in the everlasting way. (v. 24)

Lead me in your way in all of this—I am open to you and I want you! O God, help me. This all feels overwhelming. May you be holy in this, may your kingdom come in this, may your will be done. Lord, lead me into your eternal life in Jesus. Amen.

Thus, the imprecation in prayer, "God blot them out, kill them," is not just an expression of anger but a turning point in our anger in which we turn over our anger to God to let him teach us in the sanctuary of prayer, to let him take vengeance, and to learn from him what is truly in the heart.

Psalm 69: A Lament or Prayer of Imprecation— Jesus's Prayer*

Psalm 69 is recognized by all as a messianic psalm. The psalm, in parts, clearly speaks of Jesus's experience. In particular, Jesus recognizes this psalm is about him and on the cross speaks part of the psalm to narrate his experience. As we pray this psalm, we pray it as those who are in Christ and are shaped by his life. Take

*All verses from Psalm 69 are NASB.

a moment to pray and listen to this in light of Jesus. Here we have a prayer that gives us some sense of Jesus praying his anger and asking the Father for vengeance. The superscription says it is a psalm of David, but the true Son of David has prayed it in its fullness. Let's start at verse 7:

> Because for Your sake I have borne reproach;
> Dishonor has covered my face. (v. 7)

For God's sake, Jesus, you became a reproach. And for us, you who were in glory opened yourself to dishonor. O bless you, my Lord. You knew this was about you as you prayed this psalm.

> I have become estranged from my brothers
> And an alien to my mother's sons. (v. 8)

Jesus, your own family did not understand you! This must have been so painful. But through this prayer you could relate to your Father in heaven.

> For zeal for Your house has consumed me,
> And the reproaches of those who reproach You have fallen
> on me. (v. 9)

Jesus, you loved the sanctuary—the presence of God—with your whole soul. You so loved God, you were so zealous for God that those who hated him sought you out to reproach and hate.

> When I wept in my soul with fasting,
> It became my reproach.
> When I made sackcloth my clothing,
> I became a byword to them. (vv. 10–11)

No one understood your life, Jesus. They did not understand someone who, so young, would feel and see the reality of things

201

and be a child and man of sorrows. O Jesus, we are all superficial compared to you.

> Those who sit in the gate talk about me,
> And I am the song of the drunkards. (v. 12)

Ridiculed by all. Oh, how hard this must have been, my Jesus. But how good it must have been to have these words written just for you, to reflect your heart to God.

> But as for me, my prayer is to You, O LORD, at an
>   acceptable time;
> O God, in the greatness of Your lovingkindness,
> Answer me with Your saving truth. (v. 13)

Yes, Jesus, you truly prayed to the Father, and you were so open to how great his love is. And in your humanity, you looked to God for salvation and deliverance in your plight.

> Deliver me from the mire and do not let me sink;
> May I be delivered from my foes and from the deep waters.
>   (v. 14)

O Jesus, this prayer was preparation for Gethsemane, to ask for deliverance from all the enemies you had and the difficulties that were constantly confronting you.

> May the flood of water not overflow me
> Nor the deep swallow me up,
> Nor the pit shut its mouth on me. (v. 15)

Yes, Lord. Even you had to ask not to be overtaken by all the trials. You were like me, wanting deliverance. Unlike me, you loved to pray to your Father. He really was your only solace.

> Answer me, O LORD, for Your lovingkindness is good;
> According to the greatness of Your compassion, turn to me,

> And do not hide Your face from Your servant,
> For I am in distress; answer me quickly.
> Oh draw near to my soul and redeem it;
> Ransom me because of my enemies! (vv. 16–18)

O Jesus, you truly prayed this prayer. You wanted the deep fellowship with your Father to be redeemed from the trials of your life and all your foes. Bless you, my Lord.

> You know my reproach and my shame and my dishonor;
> All my adversaries are before You.
> Reproach has broken my heart and I am so sick.
> And I looked for sympathy, but there was none,
>   (vv. 19–20)

As you walked to the cross, and even on the cross, you found no sympathy. So much rejection. It must have broken your heart. O Jesus, is this how you felt? Bless you.

> And for comforters, but I found none. (v. 20)

All deserted you! No one came to help ease the pain.

> They also gave me gall for my food
> And for my thirst they gave me vinegar to drink. (v. 21)

My Jesus, you knew this was about you. On the cross you recognized that you were to ask for a drink to fulfill this Scripture, as it says in John 19:28–29 and Matthew 27:34!

And now comes the anger and imprecation, the request for God to take vengeance.

> May their table before them become a snare;
> And when they are in peace, may it become a trap.
> May their eyes grow dim so that they cannot see,
> And make their loins shake continually.

Pour out Your indignation on them,
And may Your burning anger overtake them.
(vv. 22–24)

Imprecation! Anger! Jesus prayed this. Were you crying out your anger at betrayal or at their lack of faith and love? Did you translate this, then and there, into enemy love? Or was this a process you went through in sharing and giving your anger to the Father until at the right time it could be transformed into enemy love? O Jesus, what would it be to have anger like you in your humanity? I don't know. But one thing is certain: one day this prayer you prayed will come true as judgment on the wicked. O Lord, then all will truly be well!.

May their camp be desolate;
May none dwell in their tents.
For they have persecuted him whom You Yourself have
    smitten,
And they tell of the pain of those whom You have
    wounded.
Add iniquity to their iniquity,
And may they not come into Your righteousness.
May they be blotted out of the book of life
And may they not be recorded with the righteous.
(vv. 25–28)

O my, Lord Jesus. These are strong words that David and the Spirit have given you to pray, and given us to pray.

But I am afflicted and in pain;
May Your salvation, O God, set me securely on high.
(v. 29)

And here you rested in the Father, in pain, yet in the salvation of God—in the place of his protection. Bless you, Jesus, for all you went through for us.

Jesus prayed this psalm to give his hurt, pain, and anger over to his Father in heaven. Something happened over time so that this prayer of imprecation and request for God's vengeance were transformed in prayer. On the cross, on the very place of the cruelty and hatred of Jesus, he says to God, "Forgive them, for they do not know what they are doing" (Luke 23:34 NIV). Notice how anger is metabolized and transformed by prayer, experience, and life with the Father. Anger is turned into enemy love, just as Jesus talked about. Here he shows us how it is done. Somewhere in his life this was transformed. That is where our anger is going as it is shared with our Father in heaven—to forgiveness. Amen.

Psalm 88: A Lament or Complaint to God about God

Notice that the author feels entirely in the pits of life. He is overwhelmed with troubles. We don't know the nature of these troubles, but it feels to him that God has done this! He experiences these difficulties as God's anger—though we don't know the truth of the matter. It may be the same in our trials. Importantly, the pray-er is relentless in going to God. But he is struggling because he so desperately wants to be heard. When struggling, he does not hide or go to self-talk but comes to God in urgency! Bless us as we pray.

> O Lord, God of my salvation,
>> I cry out day and night before you.
> Let my prayer come before you;
>> incline your ear to my cry! (vv. 1–2)

Lord, I come before you in prayer all the time. I have not stopped, and I will not stop. You tell me to come, and I come. But please hear me in my cries.

> For my soul is full of troubles,
>> and my life draws near to Sheol.

205

I am counted among those who go down to the pit;
I am a man who has no strength, (vv. 3–4)

*O God, I have had it with life. The struggles overwhelm me. I
cannot take it anymore. I feel like my life is totally in the pits,
like I am dying. I have no strength in these times. I am overwhelmed in them.*

like one set loose among the dead,
like the slain that lie in the grave,
like those whom you remember no more,
for they are cut off from your hand. (v. 5)

*Lord, I feel totally alone in this. God, do you remember me, do
you hear me? God, I feel like I have no access to you for relief
from this trial! I am alone. God, where are you?*

You have put me in the depths of the pit,
in the regions dark and deep.
Your wrath lies heavy upon me,
and you overwhelm me with all your waves. (vv. 6–7)

*O Lord, it feels like you have put me in this trouble. You could
answer me and change this, but why don't you? Are you angry
with me? I feel like I have been the aim of your affliction—is
that true? I cannot take it anymore. I find no relief. But I come
to you. You are my only hope, O Lord!*

You have caused my companions to shun me;
you have made me a horror to them.
I am shut in so that I cannot escape; (v. 8)

*Lord, no one understands what I am going through, and they
don't even want to be around me when I am so miserable. I feel
cut off from people. God, are you behind this? Why does this
have to go on?*

> my eye grows dim through sorrow.
> Every day I call upon you, O LORD;
>   I spread out my hands to you. (v. 9)

Lord, this has gone on so long, and I feel like this trial has consumed me. But God, I come every day with my heart opened to you. I have no one else to go to who can help.

> Do you work wonders for the dead?
>   Do the departed rise up to praise you?
> Is your steadfast love declared in the grave,
>   or your faithfulness in Abaddon?
> Are your wonders known in the darkness,
>   or your righteousness in the land of forgetfulness?
>   (vv. 10–12)

God, does everything only work out when we die, when it is all over? Will this be clear then? Is there any relief in this life for your faithful, O Lord—for those who come to you in prayer? God, please visit us now.

> But I, O LORD, cry to you;
>   in the morning my prayer comes before you.
> O LORD, why do you cast my soul away?
>   Why do you hide your face from me? (vv. 13–14)

O God, I still come to you. I am invited to come, so I come early in the day that you might hear me. Lord, why are you so silent? Where are you? Lord, you could answer this prayer, you could act as you have in the past. Lord, have I done something wrong that you reject my prayers? But Lord, you say I am accepted in Jesus and I should draw near to the throne of grace. God, have mercy!

> Afflicted and close to death from my youth up,
>   I suffer your terrors; I am helpless.

207

Your wrath has swept over me;
  your dreadful assaults destroy me.
They surround me like a flood all day long;
  they close in on me together. (vv. 15–17)

Lord, this seems like it has been going on so long, and it seems like I have been here before. It has not always been like this, but Lord, this has been going on so long and it does not end. This weighs on me continually. This trial surrounds my life all the time. It never seems to be out of my mind and heart. Hear me, please. God, are you angry? Is this your way with all your children, or are you trying to teach me something? God, I don't know—please help. Lord, my prayers are becoming confusing. Help, save, pity, and defend me, Lord, by your grace.

You have caused my beloved and my friend to shun me;
  my companions have become darkness. (v. 18)

Lord, this has gotten so bad that no one wants to be around me anymore—they don't understand me. Who can, who wants to? Lord, I am so alone, and you are my only hope. I come to you. Please, please hear my cries. Amen, O Lord. Amen.

I Will Sing of the Steadfast Love of the LORD

A Maskil of Ethan the Ezrahite.

Notice: The relentlessness of prayer here, even when in great agony and confusion. We do not know if God has been angry with the pray-er, just like we may wonder this in our own lives. God's ways are mysterious. But he has also revealed himself in Christ, that we are accepted as his beloved and called to draw near for mercy. So we come in the midst of trials, confusion, and pain. We come when we feel we are thrown into the deep end of the pool and into darkness. This is prayer—raw, unfiltered, and real. This is an act of faith in the God who is there even in our darkness. This is evidence that nothing is outside of the bounds of prayer. If it is in the soul, it must be shared with God, who alone can manage and transform our souls.

APPENDIX 2

A Guide for the Prayer of Intention

The goal of the Prayer of Intention is to pray without ceasing (1 Thess. 5:17) and to present oneself to God daily (Rom. 12:1–2).

1. *Prayer of presenting oneself as a sacrifice* (Rom. 12:1–2). In this prayer, you are to present yourself to God as a living sacrifice, to open your heart to him and his will in all things for the sake of abiding in him.

> **Prayer of Intention:** "Lord, I am here. I present myself to you that I might not be conformed to the world but transformed by the renewing of the mind of Christ within me. Here I am." (Tell the Lord the truth of whether you even want to present yourself to him.)

> Leading with our intentions to present ourselves protects our wills from falling asleep to God and opens it to him right upon waking (or at any other time).

2. *Prayer of recollection* (Gal. 2:20; Phil. 3:7–9). In this time, remind yourself of your true identity in Christ (full pardon, full

acceptance) and that you are not alone because you are in Christ, and Christ is in you.

> **Prayer of Intention:** "God, whatever I do today, I want to do it in you. I have died with Christ to the law and to sin. It is no longer I who live, but Christ is now my life and he lives in me. I am fully forgiven and accepted in Christ. I don't want to live this day alone or in my own power or as a way to hide and cower. I don't want to find my identity in anything but Christ. I am in Christ, and that is my true identity." (Be open to confessing any idolatry.)

Grounding ourselves in the truth of who we are in God helps protect our lives from idolatry, false identities, and being good as a way to hide from God in prayer.

3. *Prayer of honesty* (Ps. 15:1–2; 139:23–24). Open up to God and to yourself about what is truly going on in your heart. See the truth, and take that to God in prayer.

> **Prayer of Intention:** "Lord, what is going on in my heart right now with you, with others, with my life? Search me, O God, and know my heart. Open my heart to you today in truth that I might speak what is really on my soul." (Be open to telling God whether you even want to be honest with him today.)

Offering ourselves in truth protects us from superficial obedience and closed-heartedness to God in prayer.

4. *Prayer of discernment* (Eccles. 7:13–14). Watch what the Spirit is doing in you, and don't focus merely on your work. Consider the work of God and his will, and that it is better to *cooperate* with what the Spirit is doing in our souls.

> **Prayer of Intention:** "Lord, what are you doing in my life and circumstances? What is it that you want me to become and do? What is your will for me here?" (Be open to telling God the truth of whether you really are open to his will today and in your situations.)

This protects us from responding to only our will and desires and opens us to watching for God and his will in our lives.

5. *Now, in receptivity to the Spirit, hear the Word of God.*

John 15:5, for example: "I am the vine; you are the branches. Whoever abides in me and I in him, he it is that bears much fruit, for apart from me you can do nothing."

APPENDIX 3

A Guide for the Prayer of Recollection

After you have practiced the prayer of recollection for a few weeks, you might want to add it as a kind of prayer of intention in the morning. I (John) have been doing this for years now, and I have found this particularly helpful upon awakening.

1. Right upon waking, pray the first prayer of intention as a prayer of presenting: "Lord, I am here; I present myself to you."

2. Then for the next minute or two, pray the prayer of recollection as a second prayer of intention. In just a minute, remind yourself before God who you are not. Keep in mind how the matters of your heart may cause you to trip over some of these words:

> "I am not a person who needs to be perfect at work today. I am not a person who needs to get the budget done perfectly or make that all-important sale or business deal. I am not a professor who needs to be loved by his students or a parent who needs to parent perfectly. O God, these are my concerns, but they are not me at the core."

3. Then in another minute, remind yourself of who you are in prayer. "O God, who am I? I am your beloved. That is who I really am. I am loved, forgiven, and accepted by you, even though I may not be accepted by others."

That prayer takes only one or two minutes, but it has become a real joy for me. Even when my soul betrays me and says, "Liar, you don't feel that" or "You don't feel anything," I can tell that to God in weakness and need; and in my weakness and need, I discover once again that I can do nothing apart from him.

Having used the prayer of recollection as a prayer of intention for the day, we begin the day by intending the truth with God and can do this throughout the day. As our circumstances remind us of our true identity or as we are tempted to find an identity outside of Christ, we have the opportunity again to recollect who we really are in Christ. It is not within our power to transform ourselves, but it is within our power to come honestly to the One who transforms.

NOTES

Introduction An Invitation to Love

1. Margery Williams, *The Velveteen Rabbit* (Deerfield, FL: Health Communications, Inc., 2005), 14–17.

Chapter 1 What If a Wandering Mind Is a Gift?

1. Hebert McCabe, OP, *God, Christ and Us*, ed. Brian Davies, OP (London: Continuum, 2003), 8.

Chapter 2 What If Prayer Can Be a Place to Avoid God?

1. This is the fundamental point of chapter 8 of *Beloved Dust: Drawing Close to God by Discovering the Truth About Yourself* (Nashville: Thomas Nelson, 2014).

Chapter 4 What If God Wants My Heart of Sin and Pain?

1. Dietrich Bonhoeffer, *Life Together and Prayerbook of the Bible*, Dietrich Bonhoeffer Works, vol. 5, ed. Geffrey B. Kelly, trans. James H. Burtness (Minneapolis: Fortress Press, 1996), 156.

Interlude An Invitation to Relearn Prayer the Lord's Way

1. Craig S. Keener, *The Mind of the Spirit: Paul's Approach to Transformed Thinking* (Grand Rapids: Baker Academic, 2016), 223.

Chapter 5 The Prayer Book of the Soul

1. John Calvin, *Calvin's Commentaries, Psalms 1–33*, vol. 4 (Grand Rapids: Baker Books, 2003), xxxvii; Athanasius, "Letter to Marcellinus," in *Athanasius: The Life of Antony and the Letter to Marcellinus*, The Classics of Western Spirituality (Mahwah, NJ: Paulist Press, 1979), 112. (In the original, "soul's" is quoted as "souls,'" but for readability, we have changed the apostrophe to make sense of the meaning.)

2. John Owen, *Overcoming Sin and Temptation*, ed. Kelly M. Kapic and Justin Taylor (Wheaton, IL: Crossway Publishing, 2006), 88.

3. See Walter Brueggemann, *The Message of the Psalms: A Theological Commentary* (Minneapolis: Augsburg Press, 1984). The book as a whole uses this framework to consider the Psalms.

4. While we utilize Brueggemann's framework, we are holding it very loosely and do not adhere to his overarching theology concerning this threefold movement. We have simply found it useful to name our experience in praying through the Psalms.

5. Brueggemann, *The Message*, 52, emphasis added.

6. J. Todd Billings, *Rejoicing in Lament: Wrestling with Incurable Cancer and Life with God* (Grand Rapids: Brazos Press, 2015), 45.

Chapter 6 Intending to Be with God

1. This was a comment from Dallas Willard in conversation.

Chapter 8 Being Watchful

1. It is worthwhile noting that I am not interested in articulating a Puritan account of reflection and examination. I take it for granted that the history of Christian spirituality has held, almost universally, for the centrality of these disciplines. For an early evangelical account of this, see my *Formed for the Glory of God: Learning from the Spiritual Practices of Jonathan Edwards* (Downers Grove, IL: InterVarsity, 2013).

2. One Puritan example, of many, is Nathanial Vincent, *A Discourse on Self-Examination* (Coconut Creek, FL: Puritan Publications, 2013), 223.

3. Martin Luther, *Lecture on Galatians, 1535: Chapters 1–4*, vol. 26 of *Luther's Works* (Saint Louis: Concordia Publishing House, 1963), 166.

4. We do not use the standard term *examen* for this chapter because, in some circles, it denotes a specifically Ignatian form of prayer, and we do not want to confuse the two. What we are saying here is broader and more generic.

5. We need to be careful not to overread what we just said here. We have not understood the argument of Romans until we hear what Paul is saying and declare, "What shall we say then? Are we to continue in sin that grace may abound?" (Rom. 6:1). We need to be led to that place. Of course, from there, we also need to declare, "By no means!" (v. 2).

6. Jonathan Edwards, "Letter to Deborah Hatheway," in *Letters and Personal Writings*, ed. George S. Claghorn, vol. 16, The Works of Jonathan Edwards (New Haven: Yale University Press, 1998), 94 (parentheses added for readability).

Chapter 9 Seeing Ourselves and Others in the Love of God

1. The video, with commentary, can be seen here: https://www.youtube.com/watch?v=apzXGEbZht0, accessed on August 30, 2019.

2. There is a question of whether this should be translated "in spirit" or "in the Spirit." While this is a debated point and not essential for the point we are making, it seems clear that Paul is referring to a mode of presence available in the Spirit of God and not just "in spirit."

3. For a helpful exposition of how envy works in the human heart, see Jonathan Edwards's sermon, "Envious Men," in *Sermons and Discourses, 1730–1733*, ed. Mark Valeri, vol. 17, The Works of Jonathan Edwards (New Haven, CT: Yale University Press, 1999), 104–21.

Kyle Strobel is a speaker, writer, and professor of spiritual theology and formation at Talbot School of Theology at Biola University. A popular speaker, Strobel is the author of *Formed for the Glory of God* and coauthor of *Beloved Dust* and *The Way of the Dragon or the Way of the Lamb*. He has written for *Relevant*, Pastors.com, *Christianity Today*, The Gospel Coalition, DeeperStory.com, and others. He and his family live in Fullerton, California, where he serves on the preaching team of Redeemer Church.

John Coe is director of the Institute for Spiritual Formation and professor of spiritual theology and philosophy at Talbot School of Theology and Rosemead School of Psychology at Biola University. A leading expert on spiritual formation, he is a popular speaker on the topic at churches, retreats, and seminaries across the nation. He holds three master's degrees (in Bible, theology, and philosophy) and a PhD in philosophy from the University of California, Irvine. He lives in La Mirada, California.

CONNECT
WITH KYLE

  @kylestrobel

Discover the
INSTITUTE FOR SPIRITUAL FORMATION

THE INSTITUTE FOR SPIRITUAL FORMATION at Talbot School of Theology, Biola University, is a training program in spiritual theology and formation. We are a community of faculty and students intent on growing in holiness, prayer, and ministry. Our teaching aims at understanding, maturing, and assisting others on their spiritual journey through ministries of care, spiritual direction, and a formation-informed approach to teaching and preaching. We guide students to walk in the Spirit for the sake of the church—to love God and love our neighbors as ourselves.

Visit us at **biola.edu/Talbot/academics/isf**
or follow us on **f** **@InstituteforSpiritualFormation**

INSTITUTE FOR SPIRITUAL FORMATION
TALBOT SCHOOL of THEOLOGY